WILD KITCHEN

CLAIRE BINGHAM

WILD KITCHEN

Nature-Loving Chefs at Home

280 illustrations

CONTENTS

INTRODUCTION

Green is the new black. In food culture today, the desire for eating meals that are local, nutritious and sustainable is not only for the health-obsessed. It has crossed into the realms of mainstream. People of the modern food movement – farmers, garden chefs, foragers and macrobiotic gourmands – are inspiring the world with their vibrant, fresh-looking dishes. If you are what you eat, then things are looking good. Chefs such as Alice Waters of restaurant Chez Panisse in California and slow-food crusader Maggie Beer in New South Wales, Australia, started things off. Today, the plot-to-plate aspiration has developed its own momentum, with chefs, writers, restaurateurs and social media influencers all enticing us towards delicious-looking, nature-centric meals.

It's an attitude championed by Skye Gyngell, the acclaimed Aussie chef who is known for popularizing land-of-plenty goodness at her various projects in the UK. At Heckfield Place in Hampshire, the 2-hectare (5-acre) edible garden aims to produce the lion's share of herbs, fruits and vegetables used in Heckfield's two restaurants, Marle and Hearth. This same connection to the earth is shared by Irish chef and writer Cliodhna Prendergast, who has more than a fondness for foraging the land, ideally cooking in situ. When you're cooking something in the place where the ingredient grows, or if you're cooking a fish on a riverbank, there's something very real about it. It's special.

But what does that mean for our kitchens? Despite her affinity for open-air cooking, Cliodhna's top-notch home is a food lover's dream. In this book, we step inside the home kitchens of twenty fresh-thinking chefs, who share images, stories, recipes and advice. By way of snooping inside their cabinets and asking about their favourite tools, we gain insight into a chef's style of cooking and, by proxy, their lifestyles too. As the book spirals out from London to Florence to New York to Byron Bay, each cook reveals the stories that lie behind the heart of their homes, along with a side serving of hospitality. Want to know how to organize a kitchen like a professional chef, be discerning at the farmer's market or host an informal supper club like a native Parisian? *Wild Kitchen* will take you there.

IN THE
GREAT OUTDOORS

From a house skirting the edge of a Swedish forest to a remote
Irish lakeside retreat, a wilder way of life has been embraced
by these chefs in their everyday cooking and dining.

Cliodhna Prendergast

Wood smoke and pancake feast

~~~~~~~~~

Foraging the savage, beautiful surrounds of the Connemara
National Park in the West of Ireland, Cliodhna Prendergast is an avid
gatherer of foodstuffs from this wild pantry, which she cooks either
in the open or at her contemporary lakeside home.

In the Great Outdoors

'I'm a very simple cook really,' says Cliodhna Prendergast when describing her USP. 'I try to show off individual flavours and do very little with them.' She is a modern cook with a no-frills approach, deeply linked with the outdoors, and her home suits her lifestyle. She lives in an architect-built bungalow with her husband and three children and is happiest roaming the countryside for ingredients such as spruce tips, mushrooms and seaweed. The interior is simple, with a neutral palette and natural materials. Mid-century furniture adds to the elegant vibe, but the true knockout factor is the cinematic lake view. Although the house is only a few years old, it feels like it might have existed in the woods forever.

The kitchen features a huge central island and a much-loved Aga, two things essential to the functionality of the family home. 'When you're in a professional kitchen, you need clean lines and a clear space. That's why my island doesn't have a sink or a lot of clutter,' Cliodhna explains. 'The size enables me to do commercial work, so everything has to come from there.' The Aga is something Cliodhna grew up with and, for her, it is very much the soul of the space. 'As the house is so big and modern, I wanted something warm,' she says. 'What I love most about the Aga is that you don't have to heat it up. Between family and food writing, I cook all day long, so it's wonderful to be able to open the door and throw in whatever, very quickly.'

Cliodhna cites her busy lifestyle as a factor behind the need for a certain amount of calm in the kitchen's design. There are no high cupboards, and handles are streamlined. For storage, she has a big larder that when it's open, she can see everything at a glance. The Silestone quartz countertop was chosen for its practical heat-resistant properties more than for aesthetics. 'I didn't want a busy kitchen. I wanted something that was open and organized. That's one thing about working as a chef. Every day, your job has to end. You finish your work. You put it to bed.'

But it is the woods outside where a lot of the cooking action happens. 'When you're collecting food outdoors, there's a connection with the land that's very special. When you're cooking something in the place where the ingredient grows, there's just something very real about it.'

Cliodhna's open-plan kitchen and dining area is blessed with lots of natural light streaming in through the windows, which complements her wood and limestone scheme and clean-lined aesthetic.

Tips for Foraging with Kids

#1 Even if you live in the city, you can go and pick nettles. Everyone knows what a nettle looks like and nettle soup is a good, gentle recipe for a child to have a taste of. Don't forget a pair of rubber gloves and scissors for picking.

#2 For instant gratification, try wild sorrel (pictured below). When you're walking around the woods you can pick it and eat it immediately. It tastes like Granny Smith apples.

#3 Kids love a bit of detective work, so go seaweed hunting on the shore. There's a brilliant identification flip book by Prannie Rhatigan called *Irish Seaweed Kitchen* that has all the information on each variety.

#4 Don't forage for mushrooms without an expert. Look up groups and guides in your area.

#5 Gather a few kids together for a foraging trip, so they feel as though they are on a mission.

#6 Don't forget the rules. Never clear an area of whatever you're picking as it won't come back. Never pull the root - use scissors - and use a basket for mushrooms, so they can still drop their spores.

#7 Cook outdoors. Kids love a fire - it brings a whole other dimension to what you're doing.

The woods (opposite) are very much an extended part of Cliodhna's home. 'When you're gathering ingredients from outside, it's always a pleasure to cook and eat in the same place. There's more of a thrill.' She uses her thirty-year-old skillet for cooking all sorts of things over an open fire.

Cliodhna's carbon steel knife (above) from Fingal Ferguson is one of her go-to utensils. 'Chopping with it is an absolute pleasure. I use it for everything.' Her husband bought the lava rock pestle and mortar from the market at Grand Central Station in New York.

Cliodhna likes to experiment with foraged ingredients. In the glass jar (left), she is using ground pine tips mixed with citric acid to make a sherbet dip.

She loves her Aga (opposite) most of all. 'I stand against it to get warm in the winter, it dries clothes, it's where the bread bakes, it's where you warm your toes and it's where the dogs sit. Our family life revolves around it.'

SKILLET-COOKED PANCAKES WITH SPRUCE SYRUP

Makes 6–8

Ingredients

For the spruce syrup
Fresh spruce or pine tips
500 ml (1 pt 1 fl. oz.) boiling water
500 g (17 oz.) caster (superfine) sugar

For the pancakes
100 g (4 oz.) self-raising flour
25 g (1 oz.) caster (superfine) sugar
1 egg
150 ml (5 fl. oz.) buttermilk, well shaken

Instructions
1. To make the spruce syrup, gather up some fresh spruce or pine tips and cover them, just barely, in the boiling water. Allow to steep for 24 hours for best results.
2. Once steeped, strain the water to remove the spruce tips, then add the sugar to the water and bring it to the boil, simmering it for 5 minutes.
3. Pour the syrup into a sterilized bottle with a tight-fitting lid. It can be stored for up to a month. Once opened, you will need to keep it refrigerated.
4. To make the pancakes, add the sugar to the flour and mix.
5. Separately, mix the egg with the buttermilk and whisk. Add the milk mix to the flour mix a little at a time. If you keep whisking in the same direction, you will not get any lumps.
6. Allow your batter to rest in the fridge for 30 minutes.
7. Put a pan on a medium-high heat, grease with a little oil and then rub away the excess with a paper towel. Make the pancakes in batches, pouring the batter into the pan in circles the size of a small saucer (about two tablespoons). When bubbles rise to the surface, use a spatula to flip the pancake over and brown on the other side.
8. Serve warm with the spruce syrup.

Darren Robertson

Surf and turf in Byron Bay

～～～～～～

Set within a creative community on the Australian
east coast, this sun-drenched home is a laid-back
retreat for its nature-loving family.

Chef Darren Robertson's beach house in Byron Bay is an easy-going take on the adage 'less is more'. 'We're pretty minimal,' he says. 'When we moved in the decoration was a bit daggy so we painted it and had carpenters in to build shelves out of recycled wood. The house is actually really well built so we worked with what we had. In the kitchen, a concrete bench would have been nice instead of the marble but it seems wasteful to rip it up and start again.' However, he did make a few changes to the scheme. The floors were a dark varnish, so he painted them white for a classic beachy feel, and throughout the home there are lots of natural materials, from the bamboo cloche pendants hanging over the dining table from Sydney homewares brand Koskela to the Hans J. Wegner white Wishbone chairs. It's casual, easy to live in and very outdoorsy. Bi-fold doors open up the space entirely, which is where we get insight into Darren's favourite domain. 'I dropped in a grill to cook outside and there are a couple of fire pits and a smoker too,' he says. 'We have a BBQ area, which we light at the weekends, and it's just such a lovely way to cook.'

A fan of cooking outdoors, Darren's cheffing life is a far cry from his more technical head chef days at Tetsuya, a world-renowned French–Japanese restaurant in Sydney. 'I learned so much,' he explains. 'In terms of produce, it was about getting your hands on the best stuff and doing as little as possible with it. That's the one thing that really stood with me. Back in the days of molecular gastronomy, the focus was how to make food look amazing, but the idea of sustainability has really come on now.'

Having shifted his family life to the buzzing restaurant and bar scene in Byron Bay, he runs one of the Three Blue Ducks restaurants, set on a 30-hectare (80-acre) working farm. Similarly, his own back yard is used for growing. An extension of the kitchen, this is where he lets his herbs go to seed so he can gather things like fennel pollen. 'It's dishevelled,' he admits of the laid-back vibe, but it suits the reputation of the location. With a surf break right outside the front and a spot where whales often congregate at breakfast, it's quite nice.

The kitchen-dining area is the hub of the house, with a big table designed for dinner parties and family gatherings. The table (opposite, bottom) is by Australian furniture designer Mark Tuckey and is surrounded by Danish white-framed Wishbone chairs.

Above the antique sideboard (above, right) is a rare portrait of the Beatles from the Blender Gallery in Sydney – a gift from Darren's wife, Magdalena. 'It's a pretty rare photo of them just sat around but looking happy. I'm a big Beatles fan.' She also had the chess set handmade as a gift – it is a copy of one they played with while holidaying in the Maldives.

The range (opposite) was already in the kitchen when Darren moved in, neatly positioned next to a pantry cupboard. Darren had the shelves made from reclaimed timber and uses them for storing his favourite books and a collection of soda siphons that Magdalena picked up in Buenos Aires.

The beach house is by a river and has a decked terrace area, a hanging chair and a smoker. Outside spaces are used for cooking, eating, chatting and stargazing. Darren can fish out front and the sea environment and sandy soil allow him to grow plenty of native Australian ingredients.

How I Cook at Home

#1 I'm not interested in a trophy kitchen. My dream kitchen is a big shed or a barn with an outdoor area, next to a gorgeous tree, with a fire pit and some sort of kitchen garden.

#2 I've got some really old knives from all over the world, mainly Japan - but I'm not one for collecting. If I can't fit it in my knife roll, it's not going to happen.

#3 I don't do super-fancy. I use a microplane, an old pestle and mortar. I have an ice-cream machine that holds a lot of sentimental value. It's an old one of Tetsuya Wakuda's that he used to use back in the day.

#4 I've always liked foraging. At school, I used to go on our breaks to pick nettles and dandelions. When we opened my restaurant in Bronte, I started up again with my staff. It was a nice way of showing them the ways the seasons work and what grows in the area.

#5 Marco Pierre White was my first food hero and I also love Alice Waters. She was doing what we are doing now but forty or fifty years ago. In terms of evoking conversations around food and food techniques, I also love René Redzepi's MAD Foodcamp and what Dan Barber has to say.

FARM EGGS, GREENS AND HERBS

Serves 2 adults and 2 small children

Ingredients
5 free-range (pasture-raised) eggs
3 slices of toasted sourdough bread
1 tbsp ghee
2 tbsp olive oil
1 clove garlic, crushed
1 handful of greens, such as broccoli and rainbow chard
1 small handful of baby red radishes, halved
1 handful of garden herbs, such as flat leaf parsley, fennel fronds
and oregano
Juice of half a lime
Salt and pepper
Green chili, freshly sliced (optional)

Instructions
1. Light a small fire, wash your veggies and pick some herbs while
   the fire settles. If I'm cooking this when the little ones aren't around
   I like to include some freshly sliced green chili.
2. Pop a rack over the hot coals, pour a little oil over the bread, radishes
   and greens, season with salt and cook until everything is happily
   charred.
3. In a cast-iron skillet, melt the ghee and fry off the garlic. Add the
   greens and coat in the garlic butter. Crack your eggs into the skillet
   and cook them over a gentle heat. Don't worry if you break the odd
   yolk, that sometimes happens!
4. Remove from the heat, throw over the fresh herbs and a squeeze
   of lime. Enjoy with the toasted sourdough, a cup of tea, some
   sauerkraut and pickled cucumbers.

Mette Helbæk

A Swedish fairy tale in the forest

~~~~~~~~~~

Back-to-nature retreat Stedsans in the Woods is the closest
thing you'll find to a fairy tale come true, but for its visionary founders,
it's their home and garden nearby that is real-life lived in and loved.

The best cooking is outdoors. Foraging in the Swedish forest and picking salad from her kitchen garden, Danish chef and stylist Mette Helbæk and husband Flemming Hansen have a lifestyle straight out of a Hans Christian Andersen story. Beginning their journey with Stedsans ØsterGRO, a highly successful rooftop restaurant in Copenhagen, they moved their project to the forest in pursuit of a hyper-local and off-grid dream. 'Our food reflects who we are,' Mette says of their connection with nature and desire to move out of the city. 'We went searching for the perfect surroundings for our style of cooking, which is really fresh, taking ingredients straight out of the soil and onto the plate. Vitality is such an important part of our food.'

No longer living under canvas in the woods as they did while setting up, they now base their home 20 kilometres (12 miles) away in a quiet little town called Unnaryd – a sanctuary for Mette and her three children. It is here that she raises her family, works on creative projects, tends to the garden and cooks homegrown meals. 'The move here was a law of attraction,' she says of the pretty wood-clad house that dates back to 1924. 'I was eight months pregnant, so on short deadline to find the perfect place. This house magically appeared. There's not a single day when I'm not thinking how lucky I am to live here.'

With a design that's stood the test of time, the kitchen has masses of storage, an old-fashioned pantry and shelves that go all the way up to the ceiling, for which Mette uses a ladder to reach the top spots. It may be vintage but it works well. 'It's not how you might build a kitchen today but it is effective,' she says of the functional space. The chequerboard lino, white-painted floorboards, large terracotta-potted plants and woven raffia lampshades create a relaxed feel and are distinctly Scandinavian in style. Similarly, the white walls and wood surfaces are designed to be timeless. This is a traditional setting for modern-day life.

In true Scandi style, it is a fire that is the heart of the home. Next to the kitchen is a white ceramic stove that Mette even lights up in summer. 'I prefer to cook over a fire too,' she says. 'There's something primeval about an open fire that is special. There's a continuity between generations and it makes us feel safe.' Creative, culinary and content: you could call this her happy place.

Full of original features, Mette's traditional kitchen has ample cupboard space that goes right up to the ceiling. Adding to the authentic Scandi vibe, the white ceramic stove is used – as well as for heat – to dry herbs from the garden.

Inside My Kitchen

#1 My favourite object is a grain mill for making bread (pictured right). I grind my own rye and wheat to make rye and sourdough loaves. For a chef, I'm not a huge fan of having lots of different equipment.

#2 I cook throughout the day. I like that time of day when it's five o'clock and it's okay to take a glass of wine outside and begin preparing dinner.

#3 I learned to cook from Danish cookbook authors like Camilla Plum, who are focused on the seasons and local ingredients. A more recent inspiration is Alice Waters. She is the goddess of local food in California, and I'm very inspired by that.

#4 I'm not a cheffy chef who puts on a stiff apron. I'm more of an investigator, I think. I like things to be fresh, easy, fast and intuitive.

Mette's design philosophy follows a Japanese way of thinking, where the objects she is drawn to have energy from the material they are made from, the person who cared for them and the person who made them. At home, she surrounds herself with items that fit these criteria, for instance the characterful copper pans (right) and the much-loved grain mill (above). The black and white chequerboard floor and tongue-and-groove timber-clad units (opposite) are true to the style of the modern rustic building.

Easy Cooking Outdoors

#1 Plant raised beds with different greens and herbs that you can use every day. If you surround yourself with growing things, you can pick the ingredients right next to where you cook.

#2 Consider a permanent table for prep work and a place to store a few pots and pans, so you don't need to go indoors all the time.

#3 For ultimate outdoor cooking, it's great to have running water and a basic sink.

#4 Make cooking outdoors part of your routine. While you're doing other things in the garden, you may as well start a fire.

The garden has been transformed from a plain lawn into a versatile space with raised beds, a fire pit for cooking and a greenhouse, with a decor that matches the Stedsans high-romance style.

CHANTERELLE AND POTATO OMELETTE

Serves 3–4

Ingredients
150 g (5 oz.) chanterelle mushrooms
50 g (3½ tbsp) butter
1 tsp salt
200 g (7 oz.) boiled potatoes
1 small courgette (zucchini), sliced
1 handful of kale, coarsely chopped
6 eggs
2–3 tomatoes, sliced
Black pepper

Instructions
1. Place the chanterelles into a hot, dry pan and let them cook until they release their liquid. Once the liquid is gone, add the butter and salt. Cook 4–5 minutes more, then add the potatoes, courgette and kale. Fry for another 5 minutes or so.
2. Beat the eggs and add them to the pan. Mix quickly, but not too much (you don't want the mixture to become scrambled eggs).
3. Place the tomato slices on top and cook for 6–8 minutes on a medium heat until the eggs are just cooked – again, not too much.
4. Season the omelette with black pepper, if you wish, and serve it with salad, flowers, cheese and bread.

Emiko Davies

The little Florentine kitchen

~~~~~~~~

The name Emiko loosely translates to 'blessed with beauty',
and the life of Japanese-Australian food writer and photographer
Emiko Davies certainly is. Her Tuscan home might be small but
it is mighty and showcases a passion for the Italian way of life.

Some of the best cookbooks aren't about food. They're about the story. They are a coming together of a people, a place and a history that gives a recipe its reason to be. The cookbook *Acquacotta* is all of this. It takes a trip to Maremma, a coastal area in southwest Tuscany, and transports us to a land that's far removed from the notion of lasagne and pizza. Spending six months recipe hunting and photographing the region with her sommelier husband, Marco, and their first daughter, Emiko Davies charts the landscape through the traditions of its food. 'Maremma is a nice combination of how the countryside influences the cuisine. You eat according to the seasons and what is around you. It's really clear.'

Emiko has three vital ingredients going on in her life: love, adventure and passion. Brought up between Beijing and Canberra, she also studied in the United States, but it was a semester in Florence that set her on the Italian path. Describing the experience as mind-blowing, Emiko says: 'I've always loved food, cooking, writing, and I've always loved history as well. All of those things came together in Florence, I think partly because I was exploring a cuisine that I wasn't so familiar with.' Returning to Italy after completing a fine arts degree, she started eating her way through the city, met her husband en route and began her hugely successful food blog that explores the historical connection between a dish and the place where it's from.

Home is a small two-bedroom apartment in Settignano, a tiny hillside neighbourhood on the northern side of Florence surrounded by olive groves – the kitchen feels much bigger because of all the green space outside. A self-described home cook at heart, Emiko is always in the kitchen – it's a multifunctional kitchen and living room, and also a testimony to making the most of a rental tenancy. Savvy with space, she has installed a kitchen island that serves as a table on one side with storage for pots and pans on the other. She upgraded the cabinets with a simple wood countertop to increase the food prep area and installed open shelves for utensils above. The washing machine is curtained off behind a piece of linen – in fact, the only decor to remain is the original wall tiles, which Emiko kept for their retro appeal. Relaxed and basic, this kitchen is less about gadgetry, more about traditional charm.

Most things in the kitchen are done by hand and coffee is made on the stovetop, partly as there are no electrical sockets in the space. The most technological Emiko gets is a cordless hand blender and a cordless electric eggbeater, previously having used an old-fashioned version where you had to turn a wheel.

Living in Tuscany

#1 For a lazy lunch, our spot is Caffè Desiderio in Settignano. They make lovely food using local ingredients but in a slightly different way. They also have a very nice wine list, especially wines by the glass.

#2 As we mostly cook Tuscan food, we like to drink something from the region, usually Sangiovese.

#3 Our village sits on a hill on the northern side of Florence. It's really tiny and unknown so no one visits, which is very refreshing. It's just a piazza and a couple of streets.

#4 I love the whole process of baking and the chemistry involved. I think it comes from my background in printmaking and the fact that I also like darkroom photography. In my mind, all these things connect.

#5 I love to bake while playing old Italian songs. One of my favourite singers is Mina.

Emiko's home is essentially the ground-floor servants' quarters of a villa. It's a little two-bedroom apartment that faces on to a garden and extends to an abandoned olive grove. 'The space feels much bigger because of the green space we've got,' Emiko says.

Emiko Davies   45

How I Shop at a Food Market

#1 I rarely go to the supermarket with a set list of things. I make a choice about what looks nice and decide on the spot. I buy what I can see an abundance of.

#2 I specifically go to the stalls I know, looking for signs that say *'biologico'* or *'chilometro zero'*. This means that the produce is local.

#3 I like to start my shop with an espresso and a pastry. In Florence, they make delicious little oval-shaped rice-pudding tarts in a pastry shell called *budini di riso*.

#4 Next, I buy bread. Tuscan bread has no salt in it, which is a bit strange if you're not used to it. We use it for mopping sauces, which are usually quite salty and flavourful. It's like having plain rice. The loaf is a large size but you can buy it by a quarter so you don't take home more than you need.

#5 Find a favourite fruit stall and keep coming back. The owner will tell you which are the nicest things to try.

With no room for a dishwasher, Emiko installed a sink-and-a-half (opposite) for a little bit of extra washing-up space. Above this, jars are kept on the shelves, and pots and pans beneath the island and on a trolley (right).

Emiko uses Concord or Muscatel wine grapes, fresh from the market at the tail end of summer, to make her Florentine recipe Schiacciata (overleaf). The result is wonderfully jammy, purple-stained bread that's served as a snack.

SCHIACCIATA ALL'UVA (GRAPE FOCACCIA)

Serves 6–8

Ingredients

500 g (17½ oz.) plain flour

20 g (¾ oz.) fresh yeast, or 7 g (¼ oz.) dried yeast

400 ml (13½ fl. oz.) lukewarm water

75 ml (2½ fl. oz.) extra-virgin olive oil

600 g (1 lb 5 oz.) rinsed concord grapes (or other black grapes), patted dry

80 g (4 oz.) caster (superfine) sugar

1 tsp aniseed (optional)

Instructions

1. Sift the flour into a large bowl and create a well in the centre. Dissolve the yeast in about 125 ml (4 fl. oz.) of the lukewarm water, add to the centre of the flour and mix with your hands or a wooden spoon. Add the rest of the water little by little, working the dough well after each addition, then add 1 tablespoon of olive oil and combine until smooth.

2. Cover the bowl of dough with cling film and set it in a warm place until it doubles in size (about an hour).

3. Preheat the oven to 190°C (375°F). Grease a 20 x 30 cm (8 x 12 in.) baking tin or round pizza tray with olive oil. Dust the dough with a little flour and divide into two halves, one slightly larger than the other. Place the larger half onto the pan and spread it out evenly with your fingers to cover the pan or so that it is no more than 1.5 cm (½ in.) thick. Place two-thirds of the grapes on top and sprinkle over half of the sugar, 30 ml (1 fl. oz.) of olive oil and half a teaspoon of aniseed.

4. Stretch out the rest of the dough to roughly the size of the pan and cover the grapes with it. Roll up the edges of the bottom layer of dough to the top, to seal the edges. Gently push down on the surface to create little dimples in the dough, then cover with the rest of the grapes and sprinkle over the remaining aniseed, sugar and olive oil.

5. Bake for about 30 minutes or until the dough becomes golden and crunchy and the grapes are oozing. Remove from the heat and allow to cool completely. This is best served and eaten on the day of baking, or at the most the next day.

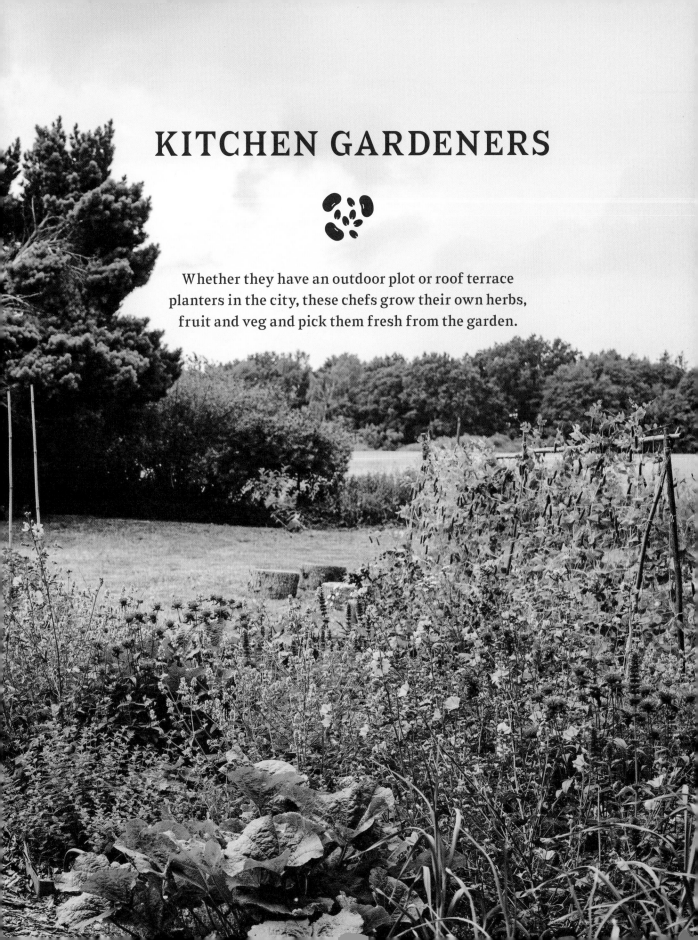

KITCHEN GARDENERS

Whether they have an outdoor plot or roof terrace
planters in the city, these chefs grow their own herbs,
fruit and veg and pick them fresh from the garden.

Krautkopf

Wood, steel and concrete

~~~~~~

A step into the past, the interior of this German settlement
house marries minimalism with a cutting-edge take
on rustic charm. For food photographers Susann Probst
and Yannic Schon it is a perfect back-to-basics refuge.

Dark and edgy with rustic accents, this no-frills hideaway is in a small village in the region of Mecklenburg in northern Germany. It is located at the end of a dirt track with open landscape all around, left deliberately low-key by its homeowners to embrace its architecture and rural surroundings. The property was built in 1948 as a settlement house: a detached house with little living space but a large plot of land that was made available to partially unemployed people or refugees for self-sufficiency, especially after the First World War. The houses, which were mostly built from recycled building materials, often included stables and ancillary buildings, as was the case here. 'It was clear that the old stable area had to become a kitchen,' says Susann. 'It was the largest and brightest room.'

Starting with a single picture on Pinterest as their cabinet inspiration, once they found the right craftsmen to implement the scheme, everything else evolved. 'We knew exactly how we wanted the kitchen to look,' says Susann. Texture was key. The couple took the building back to its bones, showcasing the beauty of raw materials. Here, primordial wood, steel and concrete work with the rusticity of the space, while the blackness of the steel and cement provides contrast against the white-washed stone walls. 'All three materials will change over the years and become more beautiful over time.'

Combining timeless aesthetics with high performance, the furniture was all custom made for the space. From the metalworker to the concrete specialist to the carpenter who crafted the cabinet fronts, the project was a collaborative effort with structural details such as the internal drawer fittings developed along the way. The cast-concrete sink and worktops are a particular design coup, while the cabinet fronts are finished with timber discovered by chance in the metalsmith's workshop. The richly grained natural wood delivers on tactile warmth, while the impressive cast-iron grills embedded in the work surface elevate the luxe factor. Consciously heading down an individual route rather than relying on design classics, the result is a kitchen quite unlike anything else.

When homeowners Susann and Yannic discovered the building it provided a creative space for them to pursue their passion for photography and food beyond the city, while enjoying the great outdoors. With its structure, texture, beautiful light and quiet setting, the house offers new inspiration every day.

The kitchen is rustic and timeless with a touch of elegance: grey monolithic blocks and industrial shelving contrast with the cobbled floor and the traditional wood-burning stove.

Inside Our Kitchen

#1 Sharp knives are our go-to kitchen essentials.

#2 Our most-loved nonessential is a hand-forged rice pot from Japan.

#3 In winter, the wood-burning stove is used to heat the kitchen. The whole house is heated exclusively with wood. During this time we also use the stove for cooking, whereas in summer it's more about gas.

#4 In terms of innovative design, our built-in gas hobs (pictured right) are ingenious. We have three rings with enough distance between each other to allow for three large pots on the go at the same time.

#5 We love new Nordic cuisine: cooks like René Redzepi, Mikkel Karstadt and Magnus Nilsson.

#6 Our favourite books include *Noma, Time and Place in Nordic Cuisine* by René Redzepi and for design inspiration, *Truck Nest* by Truck Furniture and *Wabi* by the interior designer Axel Vervoordt.

Everything was custom made for the kitchen, from the handmade cabinetry with beautiful drawer interiors (opposite) to the forged metal shelving. In the centre of the space, the high-quality cast iron and brass burners (above) are built into the work surface, with the actual hob hidden below.

The kitchen is spacious, so Susann and Yannic can cook together with others around. The direct connection to the herb and vegetable garden is a luxury for the green-fingered couple.

CARROT CAKE

Serves 8–10

Ingredients

For the cake
300 g (10½ oz.) dried apricots, finely chopped
600 g (21 oz.) carrots, peeled and grated
150 g (5 oz.) walnuts, lightly fried and chopped
6 eggs
½ tsp sea salt
225 g (8 oz.) honey
Juice and grated zest of an orange
1½ tsp grated zest of a lemon
150 ml (5 fl. oz.) of vegetable oil
375 g (13¼ oz.) wholemeal (whole wheat) flour
225 g (8 oz.) ground almonds
1 tsp of baking soda
1 tbsp cream of tartar

For the cream cheese icing
150 g (5 oz.) butter
150 g (5 oz.) icing (powdered) sugar
450 g (16 oz.) cream cheese
Juice and zest of a lemon

Instructions
1. Grease three 20 cm (8 in.) cake tins and preheat your oven to 180°C (355°F).
2. Separate the eggs. Add the salt to the whites, then beat these to form stiff peaks. Mix the yolks with the honey and add the apricots, carrots, zest, juice and oil (keep some zest aside for decoration).
3. Mix the chopped walnuts with the remaining dry ingredients, stir into the yolks and then carefully fold the egg whites into the mix.
4. Pour into the tins and bake for 40–45 minutes. Once cooked, allow to rest for 10 minutes before transferring the cakes to wire racks to cool.
5. For the icing, cream the butter with the sugar, then add the cream cheese, lemon juice and zest. Use a quarter of the icing on the first cake layer, a quarter for the second, a quarter on top and spread the remainder on the sides. Chill in the fridge for at least 1–2 hours and decorate with chopped nuts and orange zest.

Adam Aamann

Greenhouse to smørrebrød, *Copenhagen style*

~~~~~~~~

The Danish home of chef Adam Aamann exudes the same passion
for solid craftsmanship, home-grown produce and classic traditional style
for which his eponymous open-sandwich restaurants are known.

In the leafy outskirts of Copenhagen, this chic three-storey 19th-century home belongs to Danish chef Adam Aamann, his wife and three daughters. Although this would have been a summer house for Copenhageners back in the day, for Adam this strikes the right balance of city and country life. He describes living here as cosy. Cosy on a grand scale, given the size of the property, but the mood isn't at all austere.

The couple refurbished the house when they bought it, opening up the space and planting the back garden with fruit trees and edible plants. The kitchen is blessed with high ceilings, wide oak plank floors and a bank of windows that step out to the garden. 'At home, it's about really simple cooking with really good ingredients,' says Adam. 'In summer, it's wonderful to go out and grab some new potatoes and use them with a parsley butter or cottage cheese. You pick some herbs, tear them apart and that's pretty much it.'

Adam and his wife have worked to create a stylish balance between old and new, adding classic Danish furniture with lots of personal touches such as the colourful art. The kitchen and shared dining space is decorated in a soft peach, complemented by the shots of bright red and glinting copper pans.

'I wanted the kitchen to feel lived-in,' says Adam of the wood- and marble-heavy scheme that provides masses of table surface – another aspect that was key for him with the design. 'I love that my kitchen is large. I have a big sink, a big fridge, a lot of work surface and I'm able to put quite a few pots on the stove.' Factor in the generous dining table, and it means that guests can be part of the kitchen too.

Much like Adam's *smørrebrød* inventions, which are a modern take on the Danish tradition of an open sandwich for lunch, his kitchen is largely on show. 'We tried to keep everything in the open,' he says of the crockery stowed in the island and the spices lining the pantry shelves. 'When you have everything behind cabinet doors you lose a lot of time or forget about stuff. The spices, vinegars and oils – I can see all of them. I don't hide them behind a door. They can get dusty and also need to be kept tidy – but that's all part of the joy.'

Mature trees and shrubs feature in the garden of this 1850s home (opposite, top). The greenhouse is a new addition, which Adam uses to grow the basics – varieties of cucumbers and tomatoes in particular.

When planning the layout of his kitchen (opposite, bottom), the main intention was to create as much table space as possible, while retaining original features, such as the tiled chequerboard floor.

My Smørrebrød Tips

#1 For my *smørrebrød*, I like to combine unexpected flavours and textures using a huge variation of pickled vegetables and fruits to deliver a wonderful element of surprise. I've always liked the Danish tradition of lunch and *smørrebrød* is a great way of representing that. In Denmark, we are known for Nordic cuisine but this is a new invention, not so really based on our traditions.

#2 During summer, pickle elderflower in vinegar. In autumn, pickle rosehips. It's very easy and a lovely way to preserve their aromas.

#3 Space allowing, have a second fridge in the utility room or cellar. Pickling jars can take up a lot of space.

Pots and pans dangle from above, keeping the work surfaces clear (opposite). 'I like my old copper pots. These are really old French ones lined with stainless steel or tin. I love the old craftsmanship as they were made by hand.' Contemporary art and utility are happy bedfellows in the open-plan kitchen and dining room, where the guests are integral to the entertaining scene. Here, the large wooden table is surrounded by Danish Wishbone chairs by Hans J. Wegner. The brass Multi-Lite pendants are by Gubi.

Combining a leafy residential location with a period property and beautiful garden, Adam's home unites the best of classic Scandinavian design with a comfortable, easy-going spirit.

PANNA COTTA WITH STRAWBERRY GRANITA

Serves 4

Ingredients

For the granita
300 g (11 oz.) strawberries
125 g (4½ oz.) icing (powdered) sugar
2 tbsp lemon juice
150 ml (5 fl. oz.) water

For the panna cotta
500 ml (1 pt 1 fl. oz.) double (heavy) cream
100 ml (3½ oz.) caster (superfine) sugar
1 vanilla pod, split lengthwise, with seeds scraped out
3 gelatine leaves

To serve
250 g (9 oz.) fresh strawberries, rinsed and chopped into quarters
1–2 tsp sugar
8 basil leaves, finely chopped
Marigolds (optional)

Instructions
1. To make the granita, blend the strawberries until smooth and freeze them overnight.
2. To make the panna cotta, soak the gelatine leaves in very cold water. Pour the cream into a pan and add the vanilla seeds, pod and the sugar, then gently simmer for 5–10 minutes. Remove the pan from the heat once it starts to boil and remove the vanilla pod. Pour the cream into a bowl, add the gelatine (first squeeze the water from the leaves) and stir until it dissolves.
3. Sieve the cream into four ramekins and cool in the fridge for at least 3 hours until they are velvety soft, yet firm enough to turn out.
4. To serve, mix the strawberries, sugar and basil and rest for 10 minutes. Dip the base of each ramekin into a bowl of freshly boiled water and turn out onto chilled plates. Arrange the strawberries, then scrape the granita into flakes with a fork and drizzle over the panna cotta. Garnish with marigolds.

Amber Rose

True to nature

~~~~~~~~

Free-range and floral, the home of chef and writer Amber Rose
is as pretty as the food she creates. Marble worktops and a shared
dining space fit the white and airy vibe. In other words, it's chill.

The adage 'the apple doesn't fall far from the tree' couldn't be truer for New Zealand chef, writer and stylist Amber Rose. One of four siblings, she grew up in a garden where twenty-five different varieties of tomatoes was standard. At age nine, she was a literal butterfly, busy with a paintbrush hand-pollinating tomato flowers that were isolated under nets.

Amber comes from a family that was obsessed with growing and food. On her mother's 160-hectare (400-acre) farm an hour north of Auckland, they made their own bread, milked cows, made yoghurt and cheese, and kept bees for honey. Most of all, they grew. Her mother spent forty-five years cultivating the largest collection of heirloom vegetable, fruit and rare flower seeds in the southern hemisphere – all born from a desire to grow organically for her kids growing up. For Amber, the whole garden-to-table idea was instilled from an early age. 'It just snowballed,' she says of the nursery and the consequent volume of produce. 'There would be afternoons spent in mum's kitchen putting tomatoes through the press to get all the pulp or picking stalks off basil leaves that would be made into 15 litres (32 pints) of pesto. I grew up in my mum's kitchen garden and that's really where my passion for cooking also began.'

Amber worked as a food stylist and private chef in the UK before returning to New Zealand to start her own family. Home is a rural town call Buckworth Hill about ten minutes from the east coast of the North Island. True to form, her kitchen garden is very much connected to the home – Amber says she gets so much pleasure from going out to the garden and picking a handful of flowers and leaves to be added to a salad. A visual person, she extends her love for nature into the decoration too.

To create her light and simple style, Amber began by painting everything white, while keeping the floorboards bare. 'I like a soft colour palette against the grain of wood,' she says. 'The neutral base is great for food styling and for dinner parties, you can dress the space however you like.' Materials are also pared back: think marble countertops and white tiles for the splashback alongside handmade ceramics and glass. Its understated romantic style is in keeping with Amber's food photography and wildlife-rich views. Scandi chic and mid-century modern, the tableau is totally Insta-ready.

Living in a 1940s villa on the North Island of New Zealand, Amber gets her love of food from growing up on her mother's large farm and garden – a plot she recreated a few years ago and planted out with her mum's vast collection of heritage seeds. The garden here is just large enough for herbs and greens – but the love of growing lives on.

Inside My Kitchen

#1 I love to have my ceramics on display. I would feel like I was doing them an injustice by putting them behind closed cabinet doors.

#2 I'm completely obsessed with wooden spoons. I think it's the softness of the shape. I have a few spoons from Morocco hand carved from orange wood. I love the feel of natural things.

#3 My cupboard staples are good olive oil, lemons and salt. I have a 2-litre (4¼-pint) flagon of olive oil that I decant into smaller pouring bottles.

#4 When I'm cooking, I swing between quite traditional, wholesome home cooking like a good roast chicken or a healthy salad.

#5 Fruit crumble is something I make a lot that is variable throughout the season. It's a favourite with my kids.

#6 I also love a well-organized, efficient kitchen - so a good chopping board and a super-sharp knife are essential.

'I'm into natural everything,' Amber says of her simple country style. 'I love fibres like cottons, linens, silks and cashmere. I can't bear anything synthetic.' All of Amber's ceramics are either made by people she knows or have been collected on travels. The Portuguese copper still (opposite) is used for distilling various native botanicals, roses and herbs from the garden.

In the marble-topped island there are two dishwasher drawers (compact dishwashers that pull out like a drawer) and lots of storage. Pots are kept in one cupboard, frying pans in another and there's a drawer of baking stuff for all the desserts Amber likes to make. Wooden spoons, colourful ceramics, flowers, fruits and salad leaves are all a source of inspiration, and typical of the raw ingredients that Amber likes to work with.

How to Use Edible Flowers

#1 I love to use edible flowers in salads, particularly herbs that have gone to seed and have beautiful fragrant flowers, such as rocket, coriander, chive and basil. Violas, borage, calendula and even roses are also nice.

#2 Adding flowers to drinks gives colour, flavour and fragrance. Try lavender, roses, violas, pansies, jasmine, lilac, borage, marigolds and herb flowers, as well as blossom from fruit and citrus trees, such as lemon, orange, lime, apple, peach and plum.

#3 Crystallizing flowers is a wonderful thing to do for decorating cakes and baked treats. Single petals work but if you allow extra time to dry, you can crystallize an entire rose.

#4 Ice cubes with a small edible flower or petal in the middle is another lovely idea. Be sure to use boiled and cooled water for clear ice cubes to show off the flowers inside.

#5 I like to dry flowers such as daisies and violas in a flower press. After a couple of weeks they will be fully dried and can be used to decorate cakes and biscuits. Stick them in place with buttercream.

ROASTED PEACH SEMIFREDDO

Serves 8

Ingredients

6–7 yellow peaches, roughly chopped
4 large eggs
50 g (1¾ oz.) caster (superfine) sugar
¼ tsp fine sea salt
360 ml (12 fl. oz.) double (heavy) cream
35 g (1¼ oz.) coconut sugar
1 tsp vanilla powder or paste
Fruit compote of your choosing (to serve)

Instructions

1. Preheat your oven to 200°C (390°F).
2. Line a baking tray with baking paper, cover with the peaches and roast for approximately 20 minutes, then cool and blend until smooth. Transfer the blended peaches to a bowl and pop in the fridge to cool completely.
3. Pour 5 cm (2 in.) of water into a medium-sized saucepan and set it over a high heat. When the water is just barely simmering, turn the heat to low and place a heatproof bowl on top.
4. In a separate bowl, whisk the eggs with the sugar and salt until combined. Pour into your warming heatproof bowl and whisk for approximately 6 minutes or until the mix reaches 71°C (160°F) on your thermometer. Next, transfer the mix into a stand mixer and whisk until it is pale and fluffy and has doubled to tripled in size.
5. In a separate bowl, beat the cream with the coconut sugar and vanilla to form soft peaks. Take the peach mix from the fridge and fold 120 g (4 oz.) of it into the egg mixture, keeping the rest aside. Next, gently fold in the first half of the whipped cream, then the second half.
6. Line a bread tin with a large piece of cling film or baking paper, allowing an overhang on both sides. Spread one-third of the cream mix into the tin, drizzle one-third of the remaining peach purée on top and repeat to create three layers of peach and cream. Fold the cling film or baking paper over, so that the top is loosely covered, and freeze for 6–7 hours, or overnight. To serve, turn out, slice and drizzle with a fruit compote.

Julia Sherman

Cooking in colour

~~~~~~~~~

New York-born Julia Sherman, the woman who made salads
sexy, knows a thing or two about creating vibrant-looking plates.
The ability to elevate a simple salad into something inventive
and beautiful, as showcased in her immensely popular Salad for President
blog, is a skill that is echoed in the design of her kitchen – a colourful
and elegant space with a contemporary edge.

Digestion starts with the eyes – good decoration too. Harnessing the power of primary brights, Julia Sherman is a modern cook with an appetite for uplifting food – and her kitchen reflects this. Shared with her husband and daughter, this colourful Brooklyn kitchen is at the heart of her family's turn-of-the-century home. She relocated the kitchen from the basement and positioned it front and centre on the ground floor. The result is a happy social setting that stretches out to the garden below.

'Most of what drew the house to us was the original details,' says Julia. 'It was in such bad shape when we bought it but we loved the period architectural mouldings, wooden floors and big double doors. We added our personal style, which is pretty eclectic, and filled it with things we have collected over time.' Cheerful blue and yellow accents along with modern artworks make the interior feel very current, while the historic beauty of the space remains.

Given the large windows and ornate fireplace, the decision to turn a reception room into a fabulous kitchen had its own challenges. Namely, there was very little wall space for storage. This determined the need for the large island, as well as the ceiling-high cabinets that Julia steps up to with a library ladder. It also determined the suspended pot rack, so everything is right over the cooktop; and it can bear any amount of weight.

'The conversation around what materials to use was confusing,' Julia says about her choice of Carrara marble for the worktop. 'There is a lot of conflicting advice but I like the precedent marble has for being used in bakeries. It's such a classic material with a utilitarian use. I can live with the scratch marks. I've never considered the kitchen a place that should be pristine.'

She worked around other existing features such as the tiled alcove at the back of the sink. 'We added this Moroccan blue and yellow tile as a decorative splashback,' she says. 'There's no specific influence for the scheme. Instead the existing architecture makes the biggest statement and we follow from there.'

This intuitive nature marries with how she cooks her food. 'For me, it's about responding to ingredients,' says Julia. 'I can get really excited about an individual vegetable and want to make it ten different ways.' Whereas gardening is her meditation, cooking provides the fun. 'Food is about finding adventure. And if the food is actually nourishing, you can only feel good inside.'

The mix of storage ranges from the open shelving in the pantry – important to Julia so that she can see all her ingredients at a glance – to the high cabinets used for nonessentials.

Inside My Kitchen

#1 My go-to utensil is a spatula that I bought from a market in Peru. It's a crude, square cut of aluminium and a wooden handle but it's the perfect size. I love cheap utensils that are somehow ergonomically brilliant.

#2 When it comes to cooking, I like to keep things streamlined so I display only the most beautiful things in my kitchen.

#3 My fanciest kitchen gadget is a handmade Florentine kitchen knife with a beautiful inlaid handle (pictured, right). It was a present from my dad and I'm terrified to use it in case it gets ruined.

#4 I have a crazy collection of ceramics that I keep around for entertaining and sentimental purposes. I store these in my high cupboards, along with a liquor cabinet, which is nicely out of reach.

#5 I have stacks of recipe books. My favourites include Paula Wolfert's *Tagines and Couscous*, which is a deep investigation into Moroccan food and Dorothy Iannone's *A Cookbook*. It is a dedication to her lover, all hand drawn with crazy statements and interspersed with recipes.

Function is the first thing Julia considered when designing the space (opposite). The unusually large kitchen island takes up most of the footprint and gives a clue that this is a working kitchen and not just for show. The yellow bar stools and painted door add a flash of colour and excitement. The result here is like a shot of sunshine and balances with the blue-grey cabinets and eclectic decoration of the living room.

The cement tiles are custom made to match a mosaic of the same pattern that Julia loved. This was a more affordable option as the pattern is painted on.

One of Julia's favourite pieces is this handmade ceramic water filter (above, right) by Walter Filter. It's a good-looking reminder to drink plenty of water throughout the day.

Julia has a huge library of cookbooks, which she keeps the adjoining dining and living space.

Planter Dos and Don'ts

#1 Think about access. If you don't have side access to your home, then everything will need to come through the front door.

#2 Don't skimp on soil. Fill the base of a big planter with rocks and top with the very best soil. This will determine your growing success.

#3 Allow the space to dictate what you grow. A lot of city gardens will only have partial sun, so plants that need full sun, such as tomatoes and aubergines, will be a waste of time and money.

#4 In winter, try growing kale or dark leafy greens.

#5 For year-round growing, little trays of microgreens such as pea shoots or herbs are great. You only need a few centimetres of soil and a place by the window.

'We really wanted this space to work for our lifestyle,' Julia says of the back garden, which is made for entertaining and cooking outside. 'We created an enclosed feeling with a dining table and planters in a U shape.'

Julia Sherman   89

PINK PEPPERCORN CANDIED CITRUS SALAD

Serves 2–3

Ingredients

Salad
1 lemon, thinly sliced
1 thin-skinned tangerine, thinly sliced
1 tbsp caster (superfine) sugar
1 tsp pink peppercorns
3 heads of baby little gem lettuce, or Radicchio
    La Rosa del Veneto (pink chicory)
1 tbsp snipped fresh chives

Dressing
Juice of half a lemon
1 tsp raw honey
3 tsp extra-virgin olive oil
Sea salt and freshly ground black pepper, to taste

Instructions for the candied citrus
1. Preheat your broiler or grill to high.
2. Arrange the lemon and tangerine slices in a single layer on a foil-lined baking sheet. Crush the pink peppercorns using a mortar and pestle, add the sugar and grind together, then sprinkle over the citrus slices and place under the broiler for 2 minutes. Rotate the pan 180 degrees and continue to broil until they are light brown and the sugar is bubbling (3–5 minutes longer). Watch to make sure they don't burn.
3. Remove from the oven and use a spatula to transfer the slices to a cutting board before they cool. This prevents them from sticking to the foil. Once cooled, they should go from gooey and soft to chewy and almost crunchy.

To make the salad
1. Arrange the lettuce leaves in a bowl, and scatter the chives on top.
2. Combine all the ingredients for the dressing, whisking to emulsify the oil, and drizzle on top of the lettuce.
3. Season with salt and pepper and top with the candied slices before serving.

FROM FARM
TO TABLE

These chefs have set up their own farms, whether
off-site or at home, to supply fresh and sustainable produce
to their restaurants and for everyday cooking.

Rodney Dunn

A culinary pilgrimage

~~~~~~~~

Pioneer of regional dining and champion of local produce,
Rodney Dunn of the Agrarian Kitchen relocated with his
family from Sydney to transform an old schoolhouse in
Tasmania into a live–work cooking school and home.

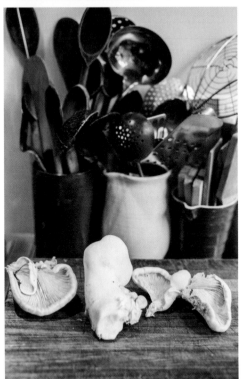

Chef, writer, farmer and teacher, Rodney Dunn has a gift for turning dreams into reality. Describing the move as a 'light bulb moment' after watching *River Cottage* one day, he woke up knowing he wanted a house and garden where he and his family could connect with nature. Switching his editor's job (and a balcony of herbs) in Sydney for a rural life on 2 hectares (5 acres) of farm, Rodney hasn't looked back.

Located in a former classroom of an old schoolhouse, the 25-square-metre (270-square-foot) family kitchen doubles up as the workspace for his cookery school. Here, he teaches people how to cook hearty, elemental feasts that are rooted in the seasons. 'I'm very lucky,' Rodney says of the huge proportions. 'I wouldn't have this amount of space if it was an ordinary home kitchen. It's lovely to have four ovens to work with, two big cooktops and that sort of thing. We always have to host Christmas, simply because we've got so much space.'

Daylight spills through the large windows, and the atmosphere is part-industrial, part-farmhouse. The key to blending utilitarian and country styles? Neutral colours and high-shine finishes. The stainless-steel units contrast with rough-hewn wood, and sleek glass splashbacks add a modern touch. 'The previous kitchen had tiles for the splashback,' Rodney recalls. 'I remember making tomato sauce one night and it splatting and staining all the grout. Instead, I opted for something waterproof.' In terms of colour, the walls are painted white behind the glass. This way, you get the natural colour of the glass, which appears greeny-blue.

The centrepiece of the kitchen is the large central bench. It's functional for the classes but works on a smaller scale too. 'As a family, we sit around the bench to eat. We cook at it. I don't think a kitchen can be too big – essentially you can never have enough space. There is the theory that the more space you have the more you spread out. It does take a little bit of cleaning but mostly only one end is ever used.'

Today, this idyllic old schoolhouse and slice of hilly terrain epitomize the diversity of Rodney's interests, which include growing vegetables, raising pigs, learning how to cure and smoke meat and even making cheese. Taking the 'farm to table' idea quite literally, everyone knows that a meal will be more delicious if you're cooking with good ingredients. Everything begins with the seed. It ends with it too.

Chef and former food editor of Australian *Gourmet Traveller* magazine, Rodney is the founder of the Agrarian Kitchen Cooking School and restaurant the Agrarian Eatery – the inspiration for which all starts in the home. 'I realized how important it was for me to be close to the source of the ingredient and where it is harvested. The cooking school is a way for me to live and practise what we do.'

Inside My Kitchen

#1 My most treasured item is my wood oven. I've cooked pizzas, bread and suckling pig in it, as well as drying tomatoes.

#2 In the living room there is a collection of about 800 cookbooks. *River Cottage* is one of the favourites, as is an American cookbook by Paul Bertolli called *Cooking by Hand*. It's beautifully written and inspirational. Over the years my collection has grown more specific. When I was a young chef, it started out all Gordon Ramsey and Marco Pierre White. Now, it's about vinegar making and curing meats.

#3 I like to listen to late '70s and early '80s music when I'm in the kitchen by myself. When the workshops are on, the music is pretty chill.

#4 The fancy stuff is our AEG steam oven. I have a vacuum packaging machine that slides out of a drawer and then you choose a sous-vide temperature.

#5 As this is an old Victorian-style building, we wanted a country kitchen look, but it had to be sturdy. I wanted stainless-steel tops to last the test of time. The patina gets better with age.

Mixing an industrial look with country, the kitchen includes items such as the old enamel light shades (opposite) that came from a friend's shearing shed. These contrast with the high-tech steam oven gear and the commercial-grade island.

From Farm to Table

Growing Advice

#1 The best place to start is herbs before progressing into the garden. If you have herbs at your back door or on the window sill it makes a huge difference to your food.

#2 Root vegetables are always a great thing to grow. One of the things that really surprised me when I started growing was the beauty of the humble carrot. In terms of sweetness, smell and taste, it's a far cry from something you could ever buy in a supermarket.

#3 Rotating crops is a lot of effort but the key thing to remember when growing vegetables is that you're trying to create amazing soil. Feed the soil and it will grow anything.

#4 Get to know your soil type. Soil can be changed and improved but if you understand it, then you will understand gardening.

#5 The highest knowledge of gardens is local knowledge. You can read all the books under the sun - but have a chat with your neighbour. Local conditions play such a large part in what you can and can't do.

At the Agrarian Kitchen, the greens from Rodney's gardens and farm are on the menu, all harvested and made à la minute. 'I wouldn't describe my cooking as very fancy. It's earthy. It's about highlighting flavours from nature and marrying things together.'

CABBAGE AND ROOT VEGETABLE SALAD WITH TRUFFLE SALAD CREAM

Serves 8

Ingredients

Salad
1 small white cabbage, quartered and finely shredded
2 large carrots, peeled and thinly sliced
1 daikon radish (mooli), peeled and finely shredded
2 turnips, peeled and finely shredded
500 g (18 oz.) brussel sprouts, trimmed

Truffle salad cream
2 tbsp apple cider vinegar
2 tsp dijon mustard
Pinch of brown sugar
125 ml (4¼ fl. oz.) extra virgin olive oil
1 tbsp single (pouring) cream
1 tbsp black truffle, finely grated
Sea salt and freshly ground black pepper

Instructions
1. Put the cabbage, carrot, radish and turnip in a bowl.
2. Bring a large saucepan of lightly salted water to the boil over a high heat, add the brussel sprouts and blanch them for 1–2 minutes. Drain them immediately and run them under cold water until the sprouts are cold. Add to the other vegetables in the bowl.
3. To make the truffle salad cream, whisk the vinegar, mustard and brown sugar together, then slowly pour in the olive oil, whisking constantly until combined. Whisk in the cream and truffle, and season to taste with salt and pepper.
4. Pour the salad cream over the vegetables and toss them until they are evenly coated. Serve.

Skye Gyngell

The female touch

~~~~~~~~~

Inside Skye Gyngell's contemporary kitchen in West London,
softness and strength are perfectly combined.

From Farm to Table

In this kitchen, there is an emphasis on simple, pared-back design. With its practical pieces that are lovingly crafted and built to last, the kitchen incorporates cabinets from British Standard (the younger, sibling brand to kitchen company Plain English), artisanal pottery and design classics such as Bestlite lamps. Blue, grey, green: there is a tonal approach that adds a serene, modern vibe. Strong materials such as marble and wood are balanced with softness and femininity. For instance, the ladylike sheer curtains in the bay window add a modern spin to retro nets. The embroidered cream linen delivers on privacy while adding lightness to the scheme. 'Air and breath is what I call it,' says homeowner and chef Skye Gyngell of her gorgeous yet sensible kitchen. 'I like shapes with space in between so that they can breathe. I feel like that with my food too. Plus, I'm a nosey parker, so I quite like to see on to the street.'

Living in what she describes as a two-up, two-down worker's cottage in Shepherd's Bush, London, Skye inverted the floor plan and positioned the kitchen at the front of the house, which to her mind was the better fit. 'The size of the rooms was quite tricky as they're not really big enough to do anything,' she explains. 'I also like that the kitchen's the first thing you walk into.' At the back of the house, a larger living room opens out to the garden and is a place for Skye to retreat to after a full-on, sixty-hour week.

A chef's life is busy. In her day-to-day life, Skye divides her time between the sophisticated country estate of Heckfield Place in Hampshire and perhaps the prettiest restaurant in London, Spring Restaurant at Somerset House. In her kitchen, she wanted to evoke a calm, relaxing mood. There is little machinery and the space is kept simple. 'There's a double sink, a six-burner stove and workspace. That's about it.'

Drawn to British Standard for their timeless aesthetic and quality craftsmanship, she says: 'I didn't want a super-sleek modern kitchen. I didn't want a Bulthaup. It's not that I don't think they can look amazing in people's houses, it just didn't feel right for me. I really like the organic nature of their kitchens and also that it's all made in England.' Given its simplicity there is something very cosy about it. Like a skirt by Margaret Howell or a pair of Church's patent shoes, some things never date.

The gardens and orchards at Heckfield Place (page 104) feed Skye's on-site Marle and Hearth restaurants. In her kitchen at home, the grey-green original floorboards and inky-blue cabinets contrast with the white marble surfaces. Skye chose her Mercury oven for its simplicity and the solidity of its design. She also wanted gas. 'I love cooking under fire. I like being able to control the heat.'

Inside My kitchen

#1 I don't have a lot of machinery. I have a gorgeous pestle and mortar and an old KitchenAid if I ever make a cake.

#2 One of my favourite things is a beautiful 1960s Danish teapot that's based on a Japanese design with a bamboo handle.

#3 My first cookbook is *Chez Panisse Cooking* by Paul Bertolli and Alice Waters. It was a gift from my father over forty years ago. When Alice came to eat at Petersham she signed it for me. It has the most beautiful photographs.

#4 I like to cook mid-afternoon, especially if I have people for dinner. I like to have things prepared in advance. During winter, I'll cook a really big soup that's full of beans that I can have a bowl of when I get home from work. I also like to eat early. I think that's from growing up in Australia. I don't like a 9:30pm appointment at a restaurant.

#5 Going to Heckfield I drive a lot, so I listen to music in the car. When I'm cooking at home, I listen to podcasts such as *The Daily*, by the *New York Times*. I also love *Table Manners* with Jessie Webb.

#6 I'm too impatient to be a pastry chef - it's much more precise - but I adore sweet things. I really enjoy the ideas behind the dishes.

Skye's books stand out on natural wooden shelves underneath the dark-blue-painted island.

A fan of beautiful ceramics, Skye uses this onggi pot (below, left) by Prindl Pottery in Cornwall for making kimchi. The classic wall lamps (above, left) are Bestlite.

How to Cook With Scraps

#1 You definitely need the will. It's about starting to look at things in a bigger-picture way and opening your mind to trying different things.

#2 A good place to start is to buy a whole chicken. You can cook it to make a beautiful soup or chop through with vegetables. Take one thing and try to use the whole thing.

#3 Try carrot peelings to make a simple coleslaw with butternut squash.

#4 With asparagus ends, we often peel them and make a simple stock for a soup or use the peelings in a salad.

#5 When the outer sheets of lettuce get really big, throw them on the grill and toss with a Caesar dressing.

#6 Think 'the next time I buy a cauliflower, I'm going to take those leaves off, grill them and put some chilli and lemon on them and see how it tastes'. If it works with one thing you might have the confidence to do it with something else.

ELDERFLOWER FRITTERS
WITH HONEYCOMB AND SALT

Serves 6

Ingredients
250 ml (8½ fl. oz.) buttermilk
240 g (8½ oz.) plain flour
120 g (4¼ oz.) semolina
Elderflowers, trimmed to make pretty hand-sized bunches
    (roughly one head per person)
Neutral oil, such as peanut or sunflower oil, for deep-frying

To serve
Icing (powdered) sugar
Sea salt
Honeycomb

Instructions
1. Put the buttermilk into a wide, shallow bowl. Separately, combine
    the flour and semolina and tip the mixture onto a flat plate.
2. Line another flat plate with parchment or baking paper to use later
    to rest the coated elderflower heads on before frying them (next step).
3. Check the elderflower heads for bugs – tapping the flowers gently
    should get rid of them. Drop the elderflower heads into the buttermilk
    one by one, making sure that it coats the stems and blossoms well,
    then dredge them in the flour and semolina mixture. Place the coated
    elderflower heads on the parchment-lined plate until you are
    ready to cook.
4. Heat the oil to 160°C (320°F) in either a fryer or a deep pan.
5. Deep-fry the elderflower heads in batches until just golden brown,
    then drain on paper towels.
6. To serve, arrange the fried elderflower heads on plates, dust them
    with icing sugar and sprinkle them with salt. Spoon a little
    honeycomb alongside and serve warm.

Charlie Hibbert

Love of the land

~~~~~~~~~

Set in its own estate and surrounded by idyllic water meadows, farmland and orchards, the family home of chef Charlie Hibbert in the Cotswolds is truly picturesque. A palette of chalky blues and simple country furniture elevates this to authentic farmhouse chic.

There's something deliciously escapist about Thyme – described as an 'English country destination' – both in its setting and in its promise of countryside conviviality. A group of honey-coloured 17th-century farm buildings, cottages and houses set in 60 hectares (150 acres) of pea gravel drives and farmland around the Cotswolds village of Southrop, it's just so pretty. You come here to relax, eat, drink and get away. Basically, it's your dream home. A family affair born from a passion for the natural landscape, food and entertaining, Southrop Manor is the childhood home of chef Charlie Hibbert, who grew up running about the vegetable garden and cooking at home with his mum, Caryn Hibbert – the creative force and estate-builder behind Thyme.

Big, open and built for family cooking, the grand, farmhouse-style kitchen was renovated by Caryn to create a large convivial space that was well equipped and organized, yet a place where everyone could gather from breakfast to supper. It is the central axis to their busy family life. 'It's the hub of the house,' says Charlie of the living–kitchen layout. 'It's modern, chic and used all day long. There's also an Aga at the end, which is always lovely to use. I cook here especially when there are parties.'

Used to entertaining frequently, Caryn wanted the space to be multifunctional so you can cook and talk to guests simultaneously. With parts of the manor house dating back to the Domesday Book, the previous layout was composed of two smaller rooms with a hallway down the side – much smaller and darker than it is today. Having knocked down the walls to create one large space, a magnificent stone arch spans the width – not only giving good bones to the architecture but creating a natural division of space. On one side there's a U-shaped kitchen with its heavy-duty cooking island and on the other a refectory table for eats.

Benefiting from lots of natural light, the kitchen has double doors that open on to a walled herb garden. The soft-blue-painted island is offset by warm stone flooring and granite surfaces. Unobtrusive ceiling spots work well against the beams – pendants would have been too fussy. For a family that is enthusiastic about cooking, the kitchen has been organized with function in mind. It has the blissful feel of an unfitted kitchen while maximizing storage on all four walls. Something every good kitchen needs.

In the kitchen area, the island allows for all manner of food prep to be completed by many hands. There is a sink, a built-in oven and, directly in front of the Aga, a butcher's block for the heavy-duty chopping – performed using Charlie's collection of knives.

Inside My Kitchen

#1 I don't use many gadgets. Wooden spoons are my essential, as are decent knives and chopping boards.

#2 For knives, I love Blenheim Forge - a lot of chefs use them in the kitchen.

#3 A fried egg is my favourite breakfast at home. I cook it with oil, slowly on a medium heat so it doesn't go crispy on the outside, and serve with salt and pepper.

#4 The cookbooks I like to flick through include anything by the River Café or Alice Waters. Their cooking philosophies are the same as what was drilled into me at Quo Vadis: simple, home grown and ingredient-led. My mum's favourite is one of the original cookbooks by Delia Smith.

#5 A quick tomato salad is my favourite thing to have at home for lunch. I like fleshy tomatoes such as San Marzano, chopped with capers, sliced shallots, salt and pepper. You don't need anything else in there but could add roasted courgette and onions.

Home for Charlie is cooking for friends. His cooking is ingredient-led and simple. He describes the food at Thyme's Ox Barn restaurant as an elevated version of home cooking.

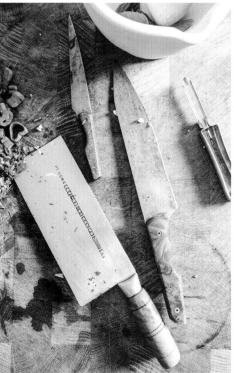

Cooking More Sustainably

#1 It starts with thinking about what you buy. Have a bit of forethought so you are buying with intent.

#2 To help reduce waste, avoid items wrapped in single-use plastic. Farmers markets are great for this. Instead, use reusable containers with beeswax wraps and silicone lids.

#3 Try to use the parts of ingredients that are usually thrown away. For instance use carrot tops for pesto, the end of vegetables for stock, and if you have a roast chicken, use the bones for soup, adding vegetables.

#4 It's important to know what you have in your kitchen. Get into the habit of rummaging through the back of cupboards and finding the packet of lentils that's been ignored.

#5 Only refrigerate what you need to. Eggs can be kept on the counter, lemons as well.

Inspired by the landscape and values of the countryside, a love of heritage and sustainable food production is the cornerstone at Thyme. All the produce for the restaurant is grown on the 1-hectare (2½-acre) kitchen garden and anything they can't grow is sourced through local suppliers.

COD, BABY LEEKS, COCO BEANS AND PANCETTA

Serves 6

Ingredients
500 g (18 oz.) fresh coco or cannellini beans
100 g (4 oz.) pancetta
2 fresh onions, with tops intact
2 sticks of celery
1 fennel bulb, chopped into quarters
5 baby leeks
Small rolled-up bunch of hard herbs, such as rosemary, thyme or oregano
6 x 150 g (5 oz.) skin-on cod fillets
1 bunch of parsley, finely chopped
Best extra-virgin olive oil
A squeeze of lemon

Instructions
1. Pod the beans and cover them with cold water, then add the hard herbs, an onion and the celery and fennel.
2. Place a cartouche over the beans – they should not peak out of the broth – and bring to a gentle simmer on a medium heat. Cook until soft but unbroken (around 35–40 minutes).
3. Gently remove the skin from the pancetta using a boning knife, then dice and place in a flat pan on a medium heat to render some of the fat from the meat. Next, dice the remaining onion (keeping the tops for later) and sweat this down with the pancetta, for around 4–5 minutes with a lid on, until soft and translucent.
4. Slice the leeks and onion tops. When your beans are ready, place the cod skin-side-up in a pan, ensuring you have a lid that fits. Pour some cold water into the pan to reach about a third to halfway up the fish.
5. Scatter in the leeks and cook on a medium heat, not allowing the pan to boil. It should take 4–5 minutes for the cod to cook through – depending on size. Test with a skewer – there should be no resistance from the fish.
6. Lift the cod out of the broth and place to one side. Stir the beans, onion, pancetta, parsley and half a handful of the onion tops into the broth, then pour into a large flat sharing bowl and rest the cod on top. Drizzle with olive oil and a squeeze of lemon and serve immediately.

Palisa Anderson

Salt of the earth

~~~~~~~

Polished concrete, salvaged timber, ceramics
and eucalyptus-inspired tiles form a tactile, natural
palette in this modern rustic kitchen.

With her eco-minded home and fertile, rainforest surrounds, Palisa Anderson is a poster girl for using natural produce. Even when living in major cities around the world, she would grow her own ingredients and go foraging for food. Today, she has scaled up her balcony garden and lives with her family on a 46-hectare (113-acre) farm – an idea born out of wanting to grow specialist Thai ingredients for her family's chain of restaurants in Sydney. Finding the land was the easy part. As the garden flourished, transforming the farm building into a family home came next.

Local interior designer Genine Noakes was hired to help Palisa with the renovation of the property on the farm – previously a farm workers' building that was unlived in. They started by opening up the windows and removing the existing floor tiles. 'It looked literally like a bathroom,' Palisa says of the original decor. 'It was a kit home with tiny little windows and white ceramic tiles on the floor.'

Drawn to Genine's warm and organic aesthetic, the kitchen serves up so much personality in its use of materiality. After stripping back the white tiles, concrete was discovered underneath – this was polished up and paired with a poured concrete island, complemented with the characterful timber for the cabinets and cooker hood. 'Everything was built with second-hand materials,' Palisa says of the natural vibe, which was created on a budget. 'The tiles are hand painted to reflect the outside environment. We have a lot of eucalyptus, so the inspiration came from that.'

Describing her kitchen as a mish-mash of styles, she has mixed salvaged materials with high-street furniture and designer lighting buys such as the oversized copper Galileo dome pendants from Italian brand Il Fanale hanging over the teak dining table. The table was found at auction and then customized with new legs. You can tell there is design savvy at Palisa's heart. 'My brother's actually an architect,' she explains. 'I grew up looking at design books and within our creative household I learned to see things with a different eye.' Living in London and Tokyo has also influenced her taste. 'I love the Japanese thing. I also love mid-century design. Saying that, when I accumulate things, I really have to love an object. When you love something, you don't mind spending the money – but it has to spark joy.'

The polished concrete flooring is one of the few features left from the original house. It melds with the poured concrete island and worktops in the open-plan kitchen area. The shelving is crafted from reclaimed wood and the tiles are hand glazed.

Top Tips for Salvage Style

#1 The biggest criterion for me was that I didn't want to use anything toxic. The good thing about using reclaimed materials is that a lot of the toxicity has gone - but find out how it has been stored. You don't want anything contaminating the food.

#2 Work with job lots of material and use it in different ways. The timber here is all from old picket fences - used to clad the cabinet fronts, the extractor fan and as shelves.

#3 Cost of installation can be high, so learning how to DIY or maintain a material yourself always helps. Yes, an IKEA kitchen is more cost-effective, but you will love this infinitely more because it has meaning.

#4 Think about your layout. My kitchen works as I can pivot in two seconds and be where I need to be.

The produce in this kitchen is laden with Thai flavours, stocked high with a multitude of wonderful organic Asian greens produced on the farm. Chive flowers, pea shoots, galangal, kaffir lime – all are grown and enjoyed from the source.

Mandarins and pomelo are displayed in a burl wood bowl turned by master craftsman Jerry Kermode of California (right).

Palisa organically grows fruits and vegetables to supply the produce for her family's Chat Thai restaurants. In the orchard, produce includes delicious Nagisakiwase loquats, known as Nagisakiwase *biwa* in Japanese, and beautiful Byron Sunrise finger limes.

Everything in Palisa's kitchen has meaning, from the pottery that she has collected over the years (opposite and below), mostly from Japan, to her next-level pestle and mortar, which is from Thailand (she has about seven). The shelves are filled, but in true chef style she prefers to keep her worktops clear.

Palisa hardly ever uses her dishwasher for washing up (below, left). Instead, she uses it for rinsing her veggies. 'It's an expensive colander but comes in handy as our space is quite limited by the sink.'

BOON LUCK FARM ORGANICS WINTER SALAD

Serves 4

Ingredients

For the dressing
2 chilis, finely chopped
2 coriander (cilantro) roots, roughly chopped
1 lemongrass stalk, finely chopped
5 tbsp extra-virgin olive oil
2 tbsp softened palm sugar
2 tbsp fish sauce
3 tbsp lime juice

For the salad
200 g (7 oz.) toasted organic macadamia nuts, finely sliced
1 large carrot, finely shaved lengthwise
1 stalk of celtuce peel (Chinese stem lettuce), shaved into thin discs
2 radicchio heads
10 betel leaves rolled and julienned finely
2 finger limes, split equatorially
6 flowering mustard flowers
20 young Beauregarde Snow peas
20 Beauregarde Snow pea tips
4 young Romanesco zucchini with flowers attached, split
4 young watermelon radishes shaved finely
2 large handfuls wood sorel leaves and flowers

Instructions
To make the dressing, pound the chopped chilis, coriander roots and
lemongrass into a fine paste in a pestle and mortar, then strain into a
bowl using a muslin and whisk in the olive oil, palm sugar, fish sauce and
lemon juice. Make the salad by assembling the ingredients as you prefer,
serving the dressing separately on the side.

*You can substitute any of these ingredients for equivalents that grow where
you live. Betel leaves can be replaced with any leafy green, for example.*

THE EXPERIMENTALISTS

These chefs like to get playful by combining healthy organic and sustainable ingredients to create exciting and unusual recipes.

Camille Becerra

Made in Manhattan

~~~~~~~~~~

Part artist's studio, part kitchen, the home of chef and restaurant
creative director Camille Becerra in New York's Lower East Side
is a place where creativity and food go together like hand and glove.
Her passion for healthy and modern food is an extension
of her lifestyle and her forward-thinking approach.

In New York, clean eating is a way of life for many – starting the day with an iced matcha latte with oat milk is standard, along with seeking out superfood, gluten- and sugar-free diets. For chef Camille Becerra, ingredients that are high on nutrition are her calling, and it is from her downtown apartment that, like a Mary Poppins of the food world, she gets to play around. She describes her home as an office and artist's studio: her kitchen and living room are a workspace where she develops recipes and takes photographs for *Domino* magazine. 'We do a lot of shoots here,' she says of the light and airy double-height living space.

When designing her kitchen, simplicity came first. Basic can be beautiful and functional as well. 'I had to renovate only because it had so much cabinetry and I wanted to open it out.' Maximizing the floor space, Camille kept to a single file of lower cabinets, with a small oven in the middle that is next to the sink. Extra storage is provided with the chef's trolleys – Camille's take-outs from working in a commercial kitchen. There is also a hanging rail for utensils so that when she is cooking, items are easy to grab.

'The oven I chose to keep small because even in a professional kitchen it's rare that you have more than four things going at one time. I wanted to be smart about having small equipment for a small space in favour of having more surface area to work on. In all honesty, it is a mix of being on a chef's salary, which is not the most profitable,' she continues. 'The trolleys are economical, plus I enjoy having things in my face. From my desk, I can see some seeds that I haven't played with in a while. It reminds me of things I want to use.'

In the kitchen, Camille enjoys that there's a good amount of light, and she likes the way it opens out to the lounge. Another highlight is the white plastered wall above the cabinets, which Camille applied in layers herself. 'It has a lovely texture that's almost like whipped cream. The colour morphs and changes throughout the day and it feels very personal.' Which is how you imagine Camille thinks about food. She experiments with ingredients and hardly ever makes the same thing twice. 'It's about going to the market and seeing what vegetables are there and creating something with that.'

With tall ceilings and fabulous light, Camille's apartment in downtown Manhattan is in a converted high school from the turn of the century. She was drawn to the neighbourhood for its old New York vibes.

'My places have always morphed into my work and the lifestyle I live,' she says on the design of her space. 'I have a lot of different spices and I play a lot with different ingredients. With the trolleys, everything is accessible.'

Inside My Kitchen

#1 I grow some of my own ingredients and my current favourite is shiso. It's delicious and tastes like nothing else.

#2 I like to cook in the quiet so I can hear the subtle noises of what the food is doing. It's nice to have music when you entertain. In my circle of friends, there's always someone that really loves to programme music, so I just get them to do it.

#3 My Columbian pestle and mortar is my most treasured object (pictured opposite). The mortar is carved out of a rock and then the pestle is a round stone that allows more control.

#4 I have a table brush that I use so much, whether it's after dinner to clean off the table or for dusting flour off a countertop.

#5 As a New York American chef, I'm not part of a longstanding tradition. I love the deep culinary heritage and simplicity of Japanese food.

#6 I use copal incense and palo santo for after dinner if I've been cooking strongly scented foods. In winter, I like adding moisture to the air with a witch hazel and lemon balm mist.

Camille has a collection of wonderful handmade ceramics from all over the world. Her pestle and mortar (opposite) are from Columbia, as is the black pot (above) – a gift from a friend, which she uses for stewing beans and other braises in the oven. It also doubles as a compost bucket. Behind this, the textured plaster wall contrasts against the smooth white Caesarstone quartz worktop that resembles Carrara marble.

Adaptogenic Herbs for Everyday Cooking

#1 I love making powder mixes with sea vegetables and lemon powder to dust over salads and rice.

#2 Steeped dried adaptogenic mushrooms make a lovely broth, which can be seasoned with smoked soy sauce and chili.

#3 Drink a little cup of cold-brewed saffron once a day. It promotes joy.

#4 My orangerie includes succulents from summer trips to Mallorca, as well as a fig and an orange tree. The rest are herbs like chervil, cilantro (coriander) and baby shiso, some chillis and tomato plants.

#5 I have a collection of Japanese tea strainers and European espresso makers, which I use to mix herb powders and make adaptogenic broths. (Adaptogenic plants are used in herbal medicine with the aim of reducing stress.)

Camille uses a commercial trolley (above) to store her spices and adaptogenic powders, which she uses to concoct her high-nutrition power-plant dishes. A wide range of spices (opposite) is used to create her adaptogenic broths.

SHISO RICE

Serves 4

Ingredients

450 g (16 oz.) sushi-style rice
270 ml (9 fl. oz.) filtered water
Pinch of salt
3 tbsp organic white sesame oil
1 tbsp vinegar
4 umeboshi plums, pitted
2 tbsp toasted sesame
1 tbsp dried red shiso condiment
4 shiso leaves, cut fine
4 sheets of nori, cut into pieces with scissors

Instructions

1. Wash the rice with cold water and drain, then combine the rice
    with the filtered water and salt in a rice cooker or pot.
2. If cooking in a pot, bring up to a boil, lower to a simmer and then
    cook for 15 minutes. Once the rice is cooked, let it rest for 5 minutes.
3. Fluff the rice, while drizzling the sesame oil and vinegar throughout.
4. Transfer onto a serving platter and dress with the remaining ingredients.
5. Serve with nori sheets, so that guests can make wraps as they wish.

Seppe Nobels

Style and substance

~~~~~~~~

Distinguished design and a calm, relaxing
mood set the tone of this Antwerp kitchen,
where the focus is firmly on nature and food.

When Seppe Nobels was a kid, he knew he wanted to be a farmer or a chef. Now one of the world's top-ranking vegetable chefs, he has done his time working in Michelin-star restaurants, yet when he opened his restaurant Graanmarkt 13 in Antwerp, he didn't want to specialize in foie gras or fancy ways with langoustine. Moving haute gastronomy in a different direction, he followed his heart instead. Here, vegetables are front and centre on the plate, fundamental to his contemporary cuisine.

It's true that you can tell a lot from a person's kitchen, and certainly a chef's. Modern, simple, with natural materials reigning supreme, this kitchen is in tune with its owner's cooking ideals. You get that there is a love of nature from the rough-cut oak cabinets and the large black-framed windows – there is so much greenery right outside the door. There is also the forest-like colour scheme of green and darkest brown. And as for the modern, this impressive kitchen takes an architectural turn with its monolithic island unit and general high-tech, high-design vibe.

Taking a heritage property and adding to an existing 1960s extension to create something excitingly new, German company Bulthaup built a kitchen marked by its clean-lined design – especially in contrast with the period features of the rest of the house. Bulthaup is known for its dark and handsome palettes and modern aesthetic, which Nobels felt a connection with. 'The house is old but I'm a chef who lives in the 21st century,' he says. 'I like the contrast. The colours aren't flashy. They're dark. I like natural materials, not artificial. This is the same for my restaurant – it's the way I think. The green terrazzo floor reminds me of my grandmother's house, so it is nostalgic for me too.'

Of course, basics are still important: there are quality appliances to cook with, but here they are all neatly hidden behind closed doors. You can see only the wooden doors and black granite topping. A gas stove is the sole appliance on show. 'In my kitchen, I work daily on induction hobs,' says Nobels. 'They are extremely fast and practical to clean, but in my kitchen at home, I wanted gas. Again, it comes back to contrast. I like the idea of seeing the flames and going back to the past. It's primordial.' As for the rest, it's concealed. Yes, there is nature – but rustic, this is not.

Embracing the darkness with a moody scheme, the cabinets are black-stained oak with the grain showing through and the work surface is a black granite. The glow comes from the dark-grey aluminium wall cabinets – a new material that's a signature for Bulthaup. It provides a lovely contrast and lightens up the space.

Inside My Kitchen

#1 There must be around eighty different herbs and spices in my pantry. I make my own Belgian pickle powder that I use for seasoning a lot but I'm not only a Belgian cook - za'atar is one of my favourite herbs. When I'm travelling I buy herbs to bring home.

#2 In a world of Spotify, I only play vinyl at home. When I'm travelling and looking for nice restaurants or herb stores, I'm also looking for rare vinyl.

#3 I scent my home all over with the terracotta pomegranates from the Florence pharmacy Santa Maria Novella. My grandfather was a wood carver and worked on the door of Santa Maria Novella. He never had the chance to see it so I like this connection in my home.

#4 My favourite utensil is a sieve in the shape of a hat that I bought from the Magritte Museum shop in Brussels. It's funny, useful and a memory of a beautiful family day.

#5 I buy a lot of vintage cookbooks to find old recipes and give them a new lease of life. I don't like to lose recipes of the past.

#6 I have many inherited pieces from my aunt in my kitchen. A kitchen is a place that you cook for people but it is also a place for memories. We don't store away our special plates here. It's all used daily instead.

Seppe's collections of vinyl, spices and books all take pride of place in the kitchen and adjoining living space. The kitchen is the centre of his home and the place where guests congregate – sometimes never reaching the dining table at all.

At the end of the kitchen, glazed windows open out to the garden, while inside, appliances are neatly hidden behind Bulthaup cabinet doors (opposite). The palette of the emerald-green terrazzo floor and black-stained oak cabinets continues the indoor–outdoor theme.

Seppe Nobels   153

SALAD OF CUCUMBER, GREEN BEANS, MUSHROOM, RED ONION, BLACK GARLIC CREAM AND ACHELSE BLUE CHEESE DRESSING

Serves 4

For the salad
30 g (1 oz.) of black garlic, peeled
1½ tsp agar agar
250 ml (8½ fl. oz.) milk
Espelette pepper
3 red onions
1 kg (2 lb 3 oz.) coarse sea salt
250 g (9 oz.) green beans
100 g (3½ oz.) field mushrooms
1 clove garlic
1 cucumber, sliced with a mandolin
Zest of a lemon, 3 branches of basil and mustard seed (to serve)

For the blue cheese dressing
80 g (3 oz.) Achelse blue cheese (or other soft blue cheese)
100 g (3½ oz.) mascarpone
Zest and juice of a lime

Instructions
1. To make the black garlic cream, add the agar agar and the black garlic cloves to the milk. Bring to the boil and season with salt and Espelette pepper. Refrigerate for 1 hour, then blend until creamy.
2. Meanwhile, arrange the unpeeled red onions in a baking dish and cover with coarse sea salt. Roast for 1 hour at 170°C (340°F). Once cooked, remove from the salt and cut each onion into 4 pieces.
3. Next, make the Achelse blue cheese dressing. Combine the blue cheese, mascarpone and lime juice and zest and whisk in a large bowl.
4. Cook the green beans in salted water, then cool them in ice water and pull each of them apart into two halves. Sauté the mushrooms in butter with a crushed clove of garlic (remove this afterwards).
5. Build the salad with the warm mushrooms on top of the beans and cucumber. Drizzle with the dressing and fill the onion lobes with the black garlic cream. Garnish with lemon zest, basil and mustard seed.

Jasmine Hemsley

Boho vibes and nutrition-rich cooking at its best

~~~~~~~~

One of the UK's most admired and popular cooks,
Jasmine Hemsley is the woman who, along with her sister Melissa,
has been at the forefront of making quinoa cool. She is cheerleader
for Ayurvedic practices and clean eating, and her 1970s home
in southeast England harmonizes with her LA state of mind.

Modern vintage with a touch of California cool, home for this green goddess is a retro, low-slung property in Kent – a recent move for the cookbook author Jasmine Hemsley and her photographer partner, Nick Hopper. The couple moved from Elephant and Castle in South London in search of more open space.

As though toying with the idea of relocating to Los Angeles, this house ticks all the modernist boxes. The format is square with lots of windows and the layout is predominantly open-plan. There are feng shui vibes throughout, which suits Jasmine's meditation; and surrounded as it is by garden, every aspect is green and lovely. 'Right now it feels like we're in LA,' Jasmine says, looking around. 'The style is laid-back, cosy yet open, and there is lots of colour.' With the dining room filled with huge plants, there's as much green inside the house as there is outdoors.

The kitchen is at the front of the house with its own cottage-style vegetable garden. 'There are three veg patches,' Jasmine says. 'We have the biggest rhubarb you've ever seen, three bay trees and a quince tree that was a wedding present from the previous owners.' An olive tree, two compost bins, lots of herbs and tomato plants add to the outdoor cornucopia.

Whereas the rest of the house is wide-open with lots of original features, the galley kitchen is small, and updated with modern materials such as the Corian work surface and built-in appliances. 'It's not the biggest space when you think of the rest of the house,' says Jasmine. 'But I've come to really love it. And as it's a galley kitchen, it's really ergonomic. It's functional and everything is exactly where you need it. I don't have to walk around to get something and it keeps me neat. I also love that it's got a sliding door. I can pull it shut without feeling too closed off.'

The oven is installed at shoulder-height, so Jasmine doesn't have to bend down to use it. There are big drawers for pots and pans and drawers for the fridge, too. 'I was used to a double American-style big fridge-freezer, whereas here, I have no freezer at all.' Rather than storing food for the sake of it, she now has minimal wastage and everything is fresh.

'I'm a creative cook,' Jasmine says of her healthy recipes that blend Eastern wisdom with Western food. 'For me, spices and herbs are nature's medicine cabinet, which is why I'm so happy to be living here with all my herbs going crazy at the back.'

For Jasmine, wellness begins at home. Her 1970s open-plan home in Kent is full of upcycled treasures, antiques and car-boot finds, which add colour and personality to the interior.

Inside My Kitchen

#1 I don't have many appliances. I have my slow cooker, which is out all the time, and I use a juicer in summer. My slow cooker is my favourite thing. It does so much of the work for me.

#2 I grow cuttings on the surface and keep homemade sauerkraut in Kilner jars on the side.

#3 I have stacks of wooden utensils, including a collection of wooden spoons from all around the world.

#4 My go-to spice tin (pictured right) is always at the side.

#5 I use raw honey on my face. It's a hundred times cheaper than any organic facemask you can buy.

#6 I have a fire pit outside that turns our home into a bit of a party house during the summer.

#7 I've learned to slow down and appreciate things I don't usually like, such as washing up. I treat it as a wind-down before going to bed.

The kitchen has two spice drawers and a spice tin, which contains her most-loved, most-used spices, including turmeric, cumin, fennel, ginger, cinnamon, coriander and cardamom. In the drawers are mustard seeds, asafoetida, garam masala and spice mixes from all over the world.

Jasmine uses her slow cooker (opposite) several times a week to make overnight porridges, stews or all-day curry.

Personalize Like a Pro

#1 Collect kitchenware from vintage or second-hand places. 'When we started Hemsley & Hemsley, Nick and I were shooting a recipe every few days. You can't just keep photographing the same bowl so we started to raid car boots and charity shops for interesting pieces.'

#2 Combine different textures, colours and eras. 'It's not like my house is absolute '70s. It's a mix of modern and vintage.'

#3 Opt for natural materials such as wood and stone. 'These items stand the test of time and age well. If something's plastic, once it's been bashed or scratched, it doesn't look great.'

#4 Choose glass-fronted cabinets instead of closed doors. This way, you get a glimpse of colour and shape behind.

A former design student, Jasmine has always had magpie tendencies for collecting old pieces. 'But not expensive things,' she states. 'Most of this stuff is from car-boot sales and junk shops. I love to give things a new lease of life. A lot of my plants are rescues. I used to live next to a commercial florist's in London, so would raid the bins all the time.' Personal touches in her modern red-and-white kitchen include her collections of vintage ceramics and mid-century coloured glassware. The 1970s wood-panelled ceiling in the dining area is original to the house.

KITCHARI

Serves 1–2

Ingredients
70 g (2½ oz.) white basmati rice
70 g (2½ oz.) mung dal (or whole mung beans, soaked overnight)
2 tbsp ghee
1 bay leaf
Pinch of asafoetida
370 ml (12½ fl. oz.) water
1 tsp cumin seeds
5 cm (2 in.) piece of fresh ginger, finely chopped, or ¼ tsp ground ginger
1 tsp ground turmeric
¼ tsp black pepper, to taste
Pinch of sea salt, to taste
Fresh coriander (cilantro), to serve (optional)

Instructions
1. Rinse the rice and mung dal three times.
2. In a heavy-bottomed pan, melt half the ghee and sauté the bay leaf and asafoetida. Add the mung dal, rice and water and simmer for 20–25 minutes, lid on, until tender. Add more water as necessary.
3. In a separate pan, make a tarka. Melt the remaining ghee, then add the cumin seeds and cook gently until they start to pop. Add the ginger and sauté until golden brown. Add the turmeric and sauté for a few more minutes.
4. Add the tarka to the rice and dal mixture. Cook for 5–7 minutes, stirring often. Season with salt and pepper and serve with fresh coriander, if desired.

Anna Barnett

An East London school turned elegant home

~~~~~~~~

Chef and writer Anna Barnett has maximized the
spatial beauty of this former school in Hackney
while adding some modern magic.

There's something about London's East End that seems innately creative. It comes from the hipster residents drawn to the buzzy bar and restaurant scene but also from the variety of buildings. As people have moved into all manner of industrial spaces and adapted them into homes, conversions are the norm. Since living in Hackney, chef and writer Anna Barnett has lived in a warehouse, an old Victorian pub, and now a former school, which means fabulous 4-metre (13-foot) high ceilings and masses of space. The interior is flooded with light thanks to the original Crittal windows that open on to the kitchen, and the mood is calm with a touch of retro thrown in – think Art Deco-style pendant lights and 1970s-inspired swivel tub chairs in luxe golden-green velvet.

When they embarked on their massive renovation, under the wing of interior design practice Studio Clement, Anna and her husband set about reconfiguring the layout, making the kitchen the focal point of the space. 'I spend most of my time here, so wanted the space to be light and bright,' she says. 'We were living in a pub before, which was very lovely but lots of stuff everywhere. This time, we were ready to pare back.'

Taking cues from Italian interiors, the decor is a lesson in simplicity, warmth and texture. Its wax-polished plaster walls echo traditional finishes from Venice, while the pink-toned elm-veneered island nods to Italian craftsmanship. The modern cabinets by London-based kitchen designers Pluck are grooved with simple handles, and an oak chevron floor adds a touch of extra detail in this otherwise minimal space. Richly veined marble countertops add to the panache. Drawn to both ends of the minimal-maximal spectrum, Anna admits that the decoration isn't entirely reduced to essentials. 'All of my stuff is eclectic and there's a lot of it too.'

What's really lovely about this home is the softness, which comes via the natural palette and also the textiles. By pairing the kitchen with a lounge area, as opposed to the dining room, the space is immediately inviting and relaxed – making the dining table all the more intimate for it. Anna's passion for cooking stems from having friends round, and the process of the build didn't quell this. Hands up to having old industrial buildings to renovate – and to the creative people who have the vision to live in them.

A masterclass in the art of mixing materials, this kitchen ticks all the right boxes. Cream-painted matt veneer cabinets combine with wax-polished Venetian plaster, and the handsome worktop in polished grey Arabescato Vagli marble is finished with beautiful brass taps by Perrin and Rowe.

Inside My Kitchen

#1 My go-to utensil is my tongs. I use them for everything.

#2 My most-loved nonessentials are a microplane and my silver salt and pepper mill.

#3 The fanciest gadget in my kitchen has to be my Miele steam oven.

#4 Nigel Slater is a food hero of mine. I'm drawn to a simplistic approach to great cuisine.

#5 Before I host a dinner party, I like a tidy kitchen. An empty dishwasher is my husband's favourite thing.

#6 My emergency dessert during the construction of my kitchen was a pineapple, Thai basil, kaffir lime and vodka granita. You just throw it all in a blender and put it in the freezer.

#7 My dream kitchen would be an old rustic farmhouse in the Italian countryside - as well as my own home.

The kitchen is at the centre of the space, next to a window, making it the brightest, best-lit area. Designed by Pluck, the island (above) is large enough to serve for Anna's cookery classes.

Keeping the decoration timeless, Anna opted for a neutral palette that could be dressed up or down. Calm, with clean lines, her style veers slightly towards the rustic with her love for antique finds. Giving a vintage Parisian feel to the space, the opaline pendant lights (opposite) are from Pure White Lines – a local London retailer.

Anna Barnett   171

Anna's Golden Rules of Design

#1 When choosing an interior designer, make sure you share a similar aesthetic or that you have a strong idea of what you would like. This way, they can interpret your taste and needs. Also make sure you have a clear budget, as costs can quickly spiral.

#2 Consider hiring a project manager. As well as keeping logistics and costs measured, the stress will be less.

#3 Seek recommendations for builders - and check in on progress daily once the project has begun.

#4 Be patient with the order of works. If you paint too soon you'll only be repainting once your builders have left.

#5 Don't rely on colour charts. Sample plaster and paint colours directly on the wall.

#6 Invest in beautiful flooring and hardware. They both make a big difference to a space.

Tucked under the mezzanine, the dining area (opposite, top) has an intimate feel, especially when guests are sat around the table. In the lounge area, the khaki velvet chairs by Molteni & Dada add warmth to the space and match the brass accessories. The marble-topped coffee table was originally a garden table, which Anna adapted with a new base.

The kitchen features two Miele hobs (opposite, bottom): induction and gas. A Miele extractor fan is built into the island beneath the oven.

Anna Barnett   173

LEMON-BRAISED BUTTER BEANS, FENNEL AND HERB SALSA

Serves 4

Ingredients
700 g (1 lb 9 oz.) giant butter beans (lima beans), rinsed
120 ml (4 fl. oz.) or 1 small glass of white wine
700 ml (1 pt 7½ fl. oz.) of vegetable stock
3 fresh bay leaves
1 lemon, halved
1 onion, peeled and halved
2 large cloves of garlic, peeled and crushed
2 large bulbs of fennel, halved, with fennel tops trimmed
and kept to garnish
Glug of olive oil
Sprinkle of sea salt flakes
Freshly ground black pepper

For the herb salsa
5 leafy sprigs of parsley, leaves picked and finely chopped
5 leafy sprigs of mint, leaves picked and finely chopped
1 tbsp capers, finely chopped, plus a splash of their pickling vinegar
½ tsp Dijon mustard
Several generous glugs of extra-virgin olive oil
Juice from half a lemon

Instructions
1. Preheat your oven to 190°C (370°F).
2. Combine the butter beans, white wine, vegetable stock, bay leaves, onion and garlic and pour into an ovenproof dish. Next place in the halved lemon and halved bulbs of fennel. Drizzle the fennel bulbs with oil and add seasoning, then roast for 30–35 minutes or until the fennel is soft and starting to darken around the edges.
3. For the herb salsa, simply finely chop or blitz all the ingredients. Taste for seasoning and adjust to your preference.
4. Serve the butter beans and fennel with seasoning, a drizzle of extra-virgin olive oil, a scattering of the fennel tops and generous dollops of the herb salsa. Serve with a crusty loaf and salted butter.

LOCAL
PRODUCE

It's never been easier to source seasonal and sustainable
ingredients in the city. These four chefs know how to make
the most of what is available on their doorstep.

Jody Williams and Rita Sodi

A taste of Italy in Greenwich Village

~~~~~~~~~

Rolling out the pasta on a desirable marble worktop, chefs Jody Williams
and Rita Sodi of Buvette and Via Carota fame have created a dreamboat
of a kitchen that mixes grand design and beautiful pairings –
with a mood that feels welcoming and warm.

A third-floor apartment between Waverly Place and Sixth Avenue is home to chefs Jody Williams and Rita Sodi. On one side there are the neon diners and traffic chaos of Waverly, on other, elegant West Village brownstones. In the middle is this showstopper of a kitchen with impeccable styling that follows the restaurateurs' legacy of high taste. This is the first home kitchen renovation for the couple, and for the aesthetic they went down a classic craftsmanship route. Cool cabinetry and quality materials, as well as super-smart organization, are the touchpoints – design courtesy of British kitchen company Plain English.

'The Italians would say it has shoulders,' says Jody of the wide-open and well-equipped space. 'It has great posture, beautiful marble, fabulous painting. As for the organization, Plain English do all these great drawers that roll out, so everything's tucked away.' Functionality is key. Broken into distinct areas, the kitchen has a cooking area, a prep area, a washing area and space to stash utility ware. There's also a cocktail station where Rita gets to play various vermouth riffs, as well as a spot devoted to making pasta. 'We have a drawer of pasta-making equipment,' Jody explains. 'We make it on the back bar underneath the cabinets, which incorporates a wooden top that slides away. We don't hang pasta to dry. Spaghetti is rolled into little nests, laid out on a cloth on the dining table. Sometimes we throw linens over a back of a chair and dry them on that.'

And then there is the open fireplace that the homeowners cherish, both for its 'simpatico' nature and for its use for cooking and smoking with embers. It's all very Italian. 'We needed a home space where we could work on our menus and entertain more,' says Jody of the crowd-pleasing elements. 'Rita's home in Florence on via Carota had a fireplace in her kitchen, so the idea came from there.'

This kitchen exemplifies the adage that 'opposites attract' – and it is something worth remembering when decorating the home. Polished materials paired with rusticity, a vibrant red and white colour palette that, saturation-wise, doesn't feel too extreme. It works like a charm. Upscale yet grounded, the veined marble, stained dark walnut floors and vintage furniture give this newly decorated home its well-loved feel.

One big space, the kitchen and dining room feature a long-length peninsula with a built-in hob. Rita's favourite spot is next to this, at the window seat, where she takes her coffee in the morning. As a backdrop to the cabinets, the bold red colour was inspired by the Waverly red-brick cityscape, and is complemented by the dark floor.

Design Details

#1 Think about what type of cook you are. If you're a baker, how do you lay out or store your baking needs? If you prep lots of veg, devote a cabinet or drawer to chopping utensils to get more enjoyment out of it.

#2 If you live in an apartment but still like a herb garden, include an area for all the maintenance. Don't leave all these special things as an afterthought.

#3 Embrace the ease of an open shelf. It's user-friendly, old-school, and you get to see the objects that you love.

#4 Don't neglect the services. Where you stow your utility brooms, cleaning products and bins is all part of the design.

Glass-fronted cabinets (opposite) and open shelves (above) form top-level storage, so the chefs' vintage glassware and Ginori porcelain can be beautifully displayed.

A signature design detail of their Plain English kitchen is a square copper sink (right). 'Rita loves it. She makes a paste of lemon, salt and flour to keep it clean. You definitely can't leave a teacup in there.'

Jody and Rita are habitual collectors and describe their affinity for objects with a narrative as a hobby. Their kitchen is full of old baskets and stools, as well as silverware and cocktail-making tools (above) — and what doesn't fit in the home goes into overflow storage or any of their restaurants. They have no qualms about buying a painting if they like it, as there is always somewhere it can go (opposite).

Commanding the kitchen space pre- and post-renovation, their refectory table (overleaf) has staying power. Rita had it shipped over from Florence and it is admired for its patina and presentation of the past.

Once the fresh pasta has been rolled out on the marble worktop, the beautiful sheets are transferred to a back of a chair where linen has been thrown over, and left to dry (left).

Jody Williams and Rita Sodi　185

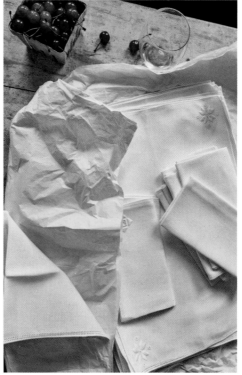

RITA'S BACELLI SALAD, GENOVESE PESTO PASTA AND BAR PISELLINO VERMOUTH SPRITZ

Serves 2

For the pesto

200 g (7 oz.) fresh basil leaves (or the leaves from 3 large bunches)
100 g (3½ oz.) pine nuts
1 clove of garlic
150 g (5 oz.) freshly grated Parmesan
70 g (2½ oz.) freshly grated Pecorino Sardo
120 g (4¼ oz.) extra-virgin olive oil
Coarse (kosher) salt (to taste)
Pasta, to serve (optional)

For the salad

60 g (2 oz.) blanched and cleaned broad beans (fava beans)
20 g (1 oz.) thinly sliced red radishes
20 g (1 oz.) sliced spring onion
4 basil leaves
4 mint leaves
20 g (1 oz.) crumbled pecorino cheese
Lemon juice, olive oil and salt (to taste)

For the vermouth spritz

75 ml (2½ fl. oz.) white sweet vermouth, Vergano
150 ml (5 fl. oz.) club soda (or sparkling water)
A lemon twist and a fresh sage leaf (to garnish)

Instructions

1. To make the pesto, blend the basil, oil, pine nuts and garlic into a paste, stopping often to push down the basil into the blender. Next, add the cheeses and salt and blend until smooth. Transfer to a small bowl and top with olive oil to store, or serve immediately with pasta.
2. To make the salad, toss the favas, radishes and spring onions in a bowl. Add lemon, olive oil and salt to taste, then chiffonnade (finely chop) the herbs into long lengths, add them to the salad and toss.
3. To make the spritz, stir the vermouth with cracked ice, top with club soda and garnish with a lemon twist and a sage leaf.

David Tanis

A moveable feast

~~~~~~~~

Hailing from the Alice Waters-Chez Panisse camp in California,
nomadic chef David Tanis moved on to Paris and more recently
to Manhattan, where he writes as a *New York Times* columnist
and cookbook author. With a focus on natural wood and crisp white
finishes – as well as simple, freestanding furniture – this kitchen
is a flexible space designed for work, rest and play.

The thing that David Tanis misses about living in California is the availability of produce year round. 'In New York, we have a real winter. There's a long spell of potatoes and onions and cabbages, so you have to cheat a little – we depend upon California as well.' A regular at the Union Square farmers market, which is closest to his East Village garden apartment, he is passionate about simple, seasonal home cooking. He is also inspired by food adventures around Europe, Asia and the Americas – evident in the objects dotted around his home.

'There's a lot of lost and found,' David says of his ad hoc homeware that makes up the kitchen scheme. 'I've done a lot of travelling and picked up things from hither and yon.' Objects range from old-fashioned Parisian grills used for toasting bread to reclaimed slate countertops he picked up on the street, relics from a school chemistry lab. One slab is used on top of the spice cabinet, the others are transformed into a splendid dining table that lives in an adjoining room. Yet the style feels nicely sparse and not cluttered at all. The white floor-to-ceiling push-open doors from IKEA are part of this sleek solution, providing masses of storage space for things David doesn't want on show.

Other design hacks include the island on castors, which was adapted by David for the space. 'Everything is handmade,' he says. 'The island was a piece of furniture that already had castors on it but we swapped the top for a longer piece of butcher's block.' With freestanding pieces, pretty much everything in the room is movable. 'The island doesn't have to stay there. The kitchen can have different configurations depending upon whether it's going to be a room full of people or just me in the kitchen alone.'

A regular at hosting private supper clubs in his previous, equally bijou home in Paris, David believes there's such a thing as too much space. 'I mean, what do you really need other than fire, water and a table? Everything else is extra. A lot of people have a trophy kitchen, especially those who don't cook very much. Here, everything is where you need it. You can't get lost.'

This kitchen shows that you don't have to go down the expensive bespoke cabinet and granite top route. Choose normal furniture instead. 'You can get stuck with the idea that the kitchen has to look a certain way. I take a more organic approach, I guess.'

The exposed stone wall has a French feel that contrasts with the plastered-cement splashback. David's heart-shaped spoon (opposite, top left) is a gift from Alice Waters and was made by a mutual friend. 'If you have a fireplace, you heat the spoon in the coals and cook an egg in it,' he explains. This is a double version.

Inside My Kitchen

#1 My style has always been minimal. This is a two-room apartment, each space only 37 square metres (400 square feet), so it's just as well. I like to hang a few things on the wall but avoid the whole collection of pans overhead. I store some in cupboards too.

#2 My glassware is kept in an old dresser and my spices are inverted in a sideboard drawer (pictured below).

#3 My fanciest kitchen gadget is the oven. It is a heavy-duty, restaurant-style appliance, bought mostly for the price.

#4 I try to avoid electric appliances as much as possible. There's nothing wrong with an electric toaster, and a blender is useful, but a food processor to me is just another thing you need to wash.

#5 I would describe myself as a spontaneous cook in terms of going to the market and seeing what looks good rather than having a fixed idea of what's going to be a meal.

David's style is a mix of old and new. The look is minimal and modern, but most of his utensils, such as his collection of pestles and mortars and wooden spoons, are second-hand. David's ceramics (opposite) are sorted into similar colours and consist of a lot of old French and Spanish dishes that work well for tray bakes. 'I don't have a problem with putting things in one vessel, but I'd rather it be a nice vessel.'

Host Like a Parisian

#1 My main approach is to keep it simple. Where possible, cook dishes in advance: include only one hot dish and avoid cooking on the stove. A simple meal could be a salad, something from the oven and finish with cheese or dessert.

#2 I like to keep the table setting casual. I sometimes use a tablecloth but my slate-topped dining table works fine with just cloth napkins.

#3 We use wine glasses with really short stems. I don't like a wine glass standing so tall over the table that when you wave your arms it's in danger of being spilled.

#4 I have a lot of silverware from French flea markets and I like to serve food on platters for guests to share.

#5 Candles make a good centrepiece. I would rather have flowers elsewhere in a room as most tables are too cluttered. We need to save room for the platter.

Mounted on castors, the oak-topped island (above) can be wheeled to another position whenever extra space is needed, making the kitchen a versatile space for entertaining.

The apartment is in the East Village of Manhattan, around the corner from old Jewish deli Russ & Daughters – the sort of place people make pilgrimages to for a smoked salmon bagel. The apartment is part of a townhouse next to an old cemetery; its stone walls are left exposed above the sink (opposite, top).

David Tanis   197

SEARED CAULIFLOWER WITH ANCHOVY, LEMON AND CAPERS

Serves 4

Ingredients
110 g (4 oz.) olive oil
3–4 anchovy fillets
Pinch crushed red pepper
2 garlic cloves, minced
Grated lemon zest
Capers, chopped
Cauliflower
Chopped flat leaf parsley
Lemon wedges (to serve)

Instructions
1. To make the sauce, heat the olive oil in a small saucepan.
2. Add the anchovy fillets and cook slowly over a medium heat until they have dissolved.
3. Add a pinch of crushed red pepper and the minced garlic cloves.
4. Turn off the heat and stir in some grated lemon zest and chopped capers. Set aside.
5. Halve and core a cauliflower and cut into small 1 cm (½-inch) thick slices. (Save the little crumbly bits for another time.)
6. Put two large cast-iron skillets over medium-high heat. Add 2 tablespoons olive oil per pan. Slip the slices carefully in the pans in a single layer. Season with salt and pepper and let them brown on the first side, 4 to 5 minutes.
7. Carefully turn them over and cook for about 2 minutes more, until tender but still firm. Don't crowd the slices or they won't crisp well.
8. Transfer to a platter, spoon the anchovy sauce over the cauliflower, and sprinkle with roughly chopped flat-leaf parsley. Serve with lemon wedges.

Rachel Khoo

Zest for life

~~~~~~~~~

A far cry from white cabinets and stainless steel,
this pretty green kitchen in London has a personality
that's as fun and fresh as its nomadic owner.

It's those little extra touches that can elevate a kitchen. Handmade glazed Mexican tiles on the wall, handcrafted brass cup handles on the cabinets, a bright-red anglepoise lamp (that happens to match your lipstick): all of these details serve up style. However, the overriding impression of this kitchen is its bolstering use of colour. It makes you want to rethink your own home's paint colours. As the trend for wellness is growing in interior design, this kitchen is very into green. 'I had a long umming and erring about the green,' homeowner and cook Rachel admits of her affection for the colour, which also matches her branding. 'I wanted something fresh. In the end, I just went for it and it was the best choice I made. Every time I look at the kitchen, it makes me feel happy.'

Rachel's gift for hosting and genuine love of cooking make her kitchen spirited, as well as beautiful. In constant use, this live–work space is used for filming, developing dishes and accommodating workshops, and as such it has to perform. Layout was key. She wanted it to be designed so that if you were shooting, you could get a view of the oven or the island and you could film straight on. There are also plenty of techy features, mainly to do with lighting. She can operate the roof windows via her phone, opening the blinds if bright sunshine needs diffusing or changing the lighting to a pink or blue tone. 'It can't be just a pretty kitchen that looks good in a magazine. It needed to be hot on working too,' Rachel says. 'Good design is not just about aesthetics, it's also about function, and when those two collide, that's when the magic happens.'

Following a complete renovation, Rachel opted for British company deVOL for the makeover – mainly for their aesthetics but also for their quality craftsmanship. 'I wanted something that was built to last,' she explains. 'I worked really hard to buy myself this property, and it was a dream come true to do up my own kitchen. I was like, okay, if I'm going to splash out, this is the kitchen: I want something to stand the test of time.'

With its own life story, the iroko worktop from Retrouvius is salvaged from an old science lab. It gives the space warmth, where a marble surface wouldn't. The tiled splashback has echoes of Rachel's former tiny kitchen in Paris – pretty patterned tiles have always characterized her homes. This time she kept the tiles simple, as the shelves above are busy with souvenirs. Paris, Sweden, London: the location of her home may vary. Her inviting style stays the same.

Updating cupboards with a lick of paint in an uplifting hue offers a fresh look that is bright and contemporary. The pea green of Rachel's shelves and cabinets is more interesting than neutral, yet not too bright, to suit the natural light of southern England.

Inside My Kitchen

#1 My heatproof silicone spatula is my go-to utensil. It's great for mixing, scraping and folding and it doesn't scratch pans.

#2 I love listening to podcasts while cooking. Some of my faves include Margie Broadhead's *Desert Island Dishes* and Dawn O'Porter's *Get It On*, where she digs through the wardrobes of her guests to reveal why they wear what they wear.

#3 My most treasured object is my yellow cast-iron pot I bought in Maison Empereur in Marseille. It weighs a ton and cost me an extra luggage fee when I brought it home.

#4 My best buy is a chef's knife I bought on my first trip to Kyoto, Japan. I even got my name engraved on the blade in Japanese. If I went back to working in a pro kitchen, no one would be able to claim it was theirs.

#5 I really like open shelves so I can curate all my bits and bobs. I can change it up and put things on display that match my personality.

#6 I've just moved and have started out growing some herbs, tomatoes and salad in the garden. We have a fabulous apple tree and lots currant bushes too.

The open shelving is one of Rachel's favourite kitchen elements, and displays a varied and ever-changing selection of bric-a-brac from her travels. Her mum's knitted tea cosy takes pride of place. The shelves are from deVOL, the blue and yellow pots are from Maison Empereur in Marseille and the paper flowers are by Pom Pom Factory in London. The Mexican glazed tiles are from Milagros.

SHIITAKE DASHI WITH QUICK-COOKED SCALLOPS

Serves 4, or 6 as a starter

Ingredients
60 g (2 oz.) whole dried shiitake mushrooms
1 tsp vegetable oil
2 spring onions, finely sliced into rounds
1 carrot, peeled into ribbons
4 scallops, roe removed and thinly sliced
1 tbsp sesame seed oil
2 tbsp of soy or tamari sauce (to serve)

Instructions
1. Soak the shiitake mushrooms in 1 litre (2 pt 2 fl. oz.) of lukewarm water for a minimum of 2 hours or, better, overnight. Strain the liquid, the 'dashi', through a fine sieve. Rinse the mushrooms quickly under cold water to remove any grit. Pat the mushrooms dry with kitchen paper and slice into thick slices.
2. Heat the oil in a frying pan. Once hot throw the mushrooms in. Fry until golden.
3. Bring the dashi to a boil. Divide the spring onions, mushrooms, carrots and scallops between the bowls. Add a dash of sesame seed oil to each bowl and pour over the boiling dashi. Serve immediately with soy or tamari sauce.

Patricia Wells

Sunny side up

~~~~~~~~~

Updating the country kitchen aesthetic with a contemporary
yellow-and-white scheme, this Parisian kitchen
and garden is keeping things fresh.

Yellow truly is the colour of happiness. It brightens up any space. From the canary-yellow Lacanche range to the ceramics on the wall, the decoration of this apartment is all about showing off what you love. 'It's just a colour I love to live with,' says homeowner Patricia Wells. 'It's happy. My home in Provence is a kind of ochre too, so it allows me to move things from place to place.'

Patricia's gift for kitchen planning (this is her tenth redecoration to date), devotion to cooking and genuine love of all things French make her 1830s ground-floor apartment as bold as it is beautiful. She teamed up with renowned Parisian property developers A+B Kasha, who specialize in the renovation of historic homes in the Saint-Germain-des-Prés neighbourhood, to create this dream kitchen and garden on the Left Bank's rue du Bac. 'If anyone is ever going to do an apartment in Paris, France, they are the best,' she enthuses of the Kashas' work. 'They have a talent that is it hard to describe.' A great friend of fellow expat and cheerleader of French cuisine Julia Child, Patricia moved to Paris with her husband more than forty years ago, swapping a journalist's life in New York for that of a food critic for the *International Herald Tribune*. It is in this apartment that she hosts her cooking school and invites people round.

The scheme for the kitchen began with the arrangement of space. Patricia knew that she wanted two sinks, a pantry area, a rotisserie and access to the garden. She amped things up with the Lacanche stove, the bright yellow balanced with the neutral tones of the marble floor, cream Silestone worktops and exposed stone walls, which are part of the original building. 'The stone is so lovely,' she says. 'It wasn't too much of a feature as the colour is soft.' The walls provide texture and the marble floors run seamlessly through the space. 'I don't like different types of floors for the living room and kitchen,' she continues. 'With a small space you need to have continuity.'

The cherry on the cake is the garden. 'Not too many people have black pepper, kumquat trees and kaffir limes growing in their garden that you can just go out and pick,' Patricia says. She is living her best life, the Parisian way.

Describing the style of her kitchen as contemporary country, Patricia hosts her cooking school from her apartment, where up to eight people will gather round the table. 'I made sure that the island was centred in the room so there was enough space between the workspace and the wall.' In the tiled courtyard, a dining table is surrounded by a collection of traditional café chairs in glorious yellow to connect with the colour scheme in the kitchen and dining room.

Inside My Kitchen

#1 My two favourite gadgets are my Lacanche rotisserie and a gas pizza oven on the terrace.

#2 I use the steamer function on my Lacanche oven every day. I have the same stove in Provence - but in red. That would have been too much here.

#3 I'm very attached to pottery that's made by people I know. All of the pottery on the wall (pictured overleaf) I bought years ago from a potter we used to visit regularly in Apt, Provence. They're all individually signed.

#4 I buy my copper pans at flea markets. I love them. I'm just glad I have someone else to clean them.

#5 My dream kitchen would have a little more space. I collect too many things.

#6 My husband does a lot of woodwork and makes my olive wood trays and chopping boards.

#7 I'm an old-fashioned girl but Julia Child is an inspiration. We built a friendship in France through cooking and food.

Hanging above the copper pans (above) is a photograph taken in 1982 by Philippe Vermes of a café in Paris called Chez Madame Gaby. 'I love Paris cafés and it was taken at the time I was just beginning to research my first book, *The Food Lover's Guide to Paris*.

Patricia's fondness for white pottery and utensils is illustrated by her collection of Le Creuset (right).

Patricia was careful to choose a shade of yellow for the scheme that wouldn't clash with the stone floor and walls. She treats her ceramics as works of art and displays them on the wall (opposite). The white plates edged in yellow are from Atelier Soleil in Moustiers.

Carefully planned storage hides equipment and utensils and there is a pull-out chopping board that neatly tucks away (above, left). There is also a warming drawer under the counter: 'You can just pull out the plates and you're ready to serve.'

Patricia gets her aprons and tea towels (left) made to order from a shop in Provence, where she has a second home. 'Owner and friend Stephanie Chatillon came up with the idea of the street sign for our logo in Paris; the same logo also appears on our cooking school aprons.'

LEMON VERBENA SORBET

Serves 12

Ingredients
100 g (3½ oz.) unrefined cane sugar
500 ml (1 pt 1 fl. oz.) whole milk
250 ml (8½ fl. oz.) double (heavy) cream
2 tbsp inverted sugar syrup or light corn syrup
25 g (1 oz.) of fresh or dried lemon verbena leaves (or about 100 leaves)

Instructions
1. To make the inverted sugar syrup, combine 450 g (1 lb) granulated sugar with 2 tsp freshly squeezed lemon juice and 250 ml (8½ fl. oz.) water in a pan and bring to a boil. Reduce the heat and simmer for approximately 8–10 minutes. Allow to cool.
2. In a large saucepan, combine the sugar, milk, cream, inverted sugar syrup and lemon verbena leaves. Stir to dissolve the sugar. Heat over a moderate heat, stirring from time to time, until tiny bubbles form around the edges of the pan.
3. Remove from the heat and let the mixture steep, covered, at room temperature, for at least an hour or overnight. Keep covered and refrigerate until thoroughly chilled.
4. Strain the mixture, discarding the verbena leaves. Transfer it to an ice-cream maker and freeze according to the manufacturer's instructions.

DIRECTORY

CLIODHNA PRENDERGAST page 10
Cliodhna Prendergast is a chef and writer who runs Lens & Larder food, literature and photography retreats with her business partner, the cook and author Imen McDonnell. She also writes a recipe column for the *Sunday Times* Ireland edition.
lensandlarder.com

DARREN ROBERTSON page 20
Chef Darren Robertson developed his cooking skills in kitchens across southeast England before hitting his stride at Michelin-starred Gravetye Manor and later moving to Australia to work with Tetsuya Wakuda. In 2011, he co-founded the first Three Blue Ducks restaurant in Bronte, Sydney, with a group of friends, which has now grown into a chain of restaurants and a 30-hectare (80-acre) farm.
threeblueducks.com

METTE HELBÆK page 30
Chef, stylist and food writer Mette Helbæk is the co-founder of eco-retreat and restaurant Stedsans in the Woods with her husband, Flemming Hansen. Mette also runs Unnaryd Apotek, where she connects people with nature via herbal teas, plant medicine and skincare.
stedsans.org
unnarydapotek.com

EMIKO DAVIES page 40
Emiko Davies is a food writer and photographer who has built a reputation for her generous stories, immersed in the rich culture of Italian food.
emikodavies.com

KRAUTKOPF page 52
Susann Probst and Yannic Schon are Berlin-based food bloggers who share their love for cooking and photography through their blog Krautkopf. Their vegetarian recipes are simple and honest, using seasonal produce to create dishes that are internationally inspired.
kraut-kopf.de

ADAM AAMANN page 62
Founder of Aamanns Etablissement, Aamanns 1921 and other Aamanns outlets in Copenhagen, chef, restaurateur and TV personality Adam Aamann is a leading figure in Nordic food culture for his reinvention of traditional Danish *smørrebrød*.
aamanns.dk

AMBER ROSE page 72
Since setting up the food blog *Wild Delicious* – also the title of her cookbook – New Zealand-based writer and cook Amber Rose has attracted an army of fans with her divine-looking dishes in perfect harmony with nature.
wilddelicious.com

JULIA SHERMAN page 82
Cook, creative director and author, Julia Sherman is the founder of Salad for President – an evolving publishing project connected with art and fresh seasonal food.
saladforpresident.com

RODNEY DUNN page 94
Chef and former food editor of Australian *Gourmet Traveller* magazine, Rodney Dunn is the founder of the Agrarian Kitchen Cooking School and the Agrarian Eatery restaurant.
theagrariankitchen.com

SKYE GYNGELL page 104
Of Heckfield Place, Spring Restaurant and Petersham Nurseries fame, Australian chef Skye Gyngell's career is characterized by her passion for natural produce. She initially trained in Sydney and then Paris before moving to London.
heckfieldplace.com
springrestaurant.co.uk

CHARLIE HIBBERT page 114
Head chef of the Ox Barn at Thyme, Charlie Hibbert grew up among a family of hosts and entertainers. He learned the importance of ingredient-driven cooking under the tutelage of Darina Allen at

Ballymaloe in Ireland and later at Quo Vadis in London, before joining the family business.
thyme.co.uk

PALISA ANDERSON page 124
Restaurateur and food producer Palisa Anderson is behind the Tyagarah-based Boon Luck Farm, a property outside Byron Bay in Australia that supplies ingredients to her family's chain of Chat Thai restaurants.
chatthai.com.au

CAMILLE BECERRA page 136
Chef Camille Becerra is the creative vision behind Café Henrie and De Maria in New York, collaborating with brands such as Apple and Google on conceptual dining experiences.
camillebecerra.com

SEPPE NOBELS page 146
Head chef at Graanmarkt 13, a high-end concept store, apartment and restaurant in Antwerp, Seppe Nobels is known for his combination of modern techniques with simple, exceptional produce that comes from the region or directly from the garden.
graanmarkt13.com/restaurant

JASMINE HEMSLEY page 156
Jasmine Hemsley is a cook and author based in the UK. Her bestselling book *East by West* (Bluebird, 2017) focuses on simple, nutrient-rich recipes for ultimate mind–body balance.
jasminehemsley.com

ANNA BARNETT page 166
Chef and food writer Anna Barnett has turned her passion for cooking for friends and family into a career with her blog Anna Barnett Cooks. She writes for several publications and regularly hosts cookery classes and supper clubs from her home.
annabarnettcooks.com

JODY WILLIAMS AND RITA SODI page 178
Chefs Jody Williams and Rita Sodi are the duo behind New York City's downtown standouts Via Carota, Buvette, I Sodi and Bar Pisellino.
viacarota.com

DAVID TANIS page 190
American chef David Tanis is the author of several acclaimed cookbooks, including *David Tanis Market Cooking*, as well as writing the weekly City Kitchen column for the *New York Times*. He spent many years as chef with Alice Waters at Chez Panisse restaurant in California. In Paris, he hosted a successful supper club from his 17th-century home.
davidtanis.com

RACHEL KHOO page 200
Cook book author, TV personality and creative entrepreneur, Rachel Khoo is perhaps best known for her debut TV show *My Little Paris Kitchen* and more recently her follow-up, *My Swedish Kitchen,* which she hosted from a traditional red Swedish cabin. After training in Paris as a pastry chef at Le Cordon Bleu, Rachel opened a tiny restaurant in her Parisian flat, where she passed on her passion for French food cooked simply, made with a modern twist.
rachelkhoo.com

PATRICIA WELLS page 208
Patricia Wells's infatuation with Paris has kept her rooted in the city for more than four decades. Combining her passions for food and journalism, her life as a cook, food critic and cookery school patron has been nurtured by the City of Light.
patriciawells.com

A NOTE ON RECIPES

All the recipes in this book give terms for ingredients in both British and US English and measurements in metric alongside US conversions into ounces, pounds, fluid ounces and pints. If you wish to convert US pints and fluid ounces to imperial equivalents, one US fluid ounce is equal to 1.04 imperial ounces and one US pint is equal to 0.83 imperial pints.

ABOUT THE AUTHOR

Claire Bingham is an interiors journalist and author who has been finding, writing about and photographing amazing homes for almost twenty years. Previously the homes editor of UK *Elle Decoration*, she writes about interiors, travel, perfume and food for publications worldwide including *Vogue Italia*, *Sunday Times Style*, *Architectural Digest* and *Grazia* (UK). She is the author of eleven design books and *Wild Kitchen* is her first book for Thames & Hudson. Originally from Yorkshire, Claire has lived in London, Milan and Sydney. Today, her home is in Cheshire, which she shares with her husband and daughter.

ACKNOWLEDGMENTS

As a journalist, it's always a privilege to dip into territories I haven't visited before. There's always something new to learn. The world of chefs (and their homes) is a fascinating one and I'm very grateful for the experience. A year in the making, my journey for *Wild Kitchen* began in Connemara, West Ireland, to photograph the home of chef Cliodhna Prendgergast. It was the starting point from where everything else followed and I can't thank Cliodhna enough for her invaluable introduction to the culinary scene. Within the book, I'm honoured to feature the NYC homes of chefs Camille Becerra, as well as Jody Williams and Rita Sodi – especially as they were photographed by legends Andrea Gentl and Martin Hyers. In Australia, Petrina Tinslay flew north from Sydney to shoot the Byron farm of Palisa Anderson and the beach property of Three Blue Duck's restaurant owner Darren Robertson. In London and across Europe, I have been blessed to work with so many talented photographers. I'm appreciative of all the effort, skill and time employed. In the production of *Wild Kitchen*, there was an awful lot of research and correspondence required across many various time zones. The process was made all the more manageable with the help of my wingman Marc Holden, with all his precious cool and calm. Finally, to all the chefs I pestered into allowing me to capture their home, merci. It was fun.

CREDITS

RECIPES
Pages 48–49: Recipe excerpted from *Florentine* by Emiko Davies (Hardie Grant Books, 2016); **Page 70–71:** Recipe courtesy of Adam Aamann; **Pages 80–81:** Recipe excerpted from *Wild Delicious* by Amber Rose (Penguin Random House New Zealand Limited, 2018); **Pages 90–91:** Recipe excerpted from *Salad for President* by Julia Sherman (Abrams, 2018); **Pages 112–13:** Recipe courtesy of Skye Gyngell, Culinary Director at Heckfield Place; **Pages 164–65:** Recipe excerpted from *East by West* by Jasmine Hemsley (Bluebird, 2017); **Pages 198–99:** Recipe excerpted from *Market Cooking*. Text copyright © 2017 by David Tanis. Photographs copyright © 2017 by Evan Sung. Used by permission of Artisan, a division of Workman Publishing Co., Inc., New York. All rights reserved; **Pages 206–207:** Recipe courtesy of Rachel Khoo; rachelkhoo.com

PHOTOGRAPHY
(T = top, B = bottom, L = left, R = right)
2, 92–93: Rich Stapleton © 2020 Thyme Southrop Manor Estate; 4, 50–61: © Krautkopf; 7TL, 7BL: Courtesy of Heckfield Place; 7TR, 7BR: Mike Karlsson Lundgren for Stedsans in the Woods; 8–18, 114–23: © Claire Bingham; 20–29, 124–33: © Petrina Tinslay; 24TR: featured image of Beatles, photographed in LA by Curt Gunther; 30–39: Mike Karlsson Lundgren; 40–49: Emiko Davies; 62–71: Styling: Rikke Graff Juel; Photography © Anitta Behrendt/Living Inside; 72–73, 78TR, 81: Claire Mossong; 74–79: Vanessa Wu; 82–91: Emily Wren Photography; 94–103: Adam Gibson; 104, 110, 113: Courtesy of Heckfield Place; 105–109, 111, 166–75: © Chris Tubbs Photography; 134–45, 178–89: © Gentl and Hyers; 146–55: Frederik Vercruysse; 156–65: Nick Hopper Photography; 176–77, 190–97: Heidi's Bridge; 199: © 2017 by Evan Sung; 200: Maria Bell © Rachel Khoo; 201–205: courtesy of deVOL; 202: boSom leP; 202BR: Laura Edwards; 204T: © Rachel Khoo; 208–17: Virginie Garnier.

INDEX

Page 2: Charlie Hibbert walking on the Thyme estate; Pages 4 and 50: Krautkopf's garden; Page 7 TL & BL: Scenes from Heckfield Place estate; Page 7 TR & BR: Mette Helbæk prepares dishes using fresh, natural ingredients at her retreat Stedsans in the Woods; Page 8: View across the lake near Cliodhna Prendergast's home; Page 92: The kitchen garden at Thyme; Page 134: Camille Becerra's crockery; Page 176: David Tanis's kitchen.

First published in the United Kingdom in 2020
by Thames & Hudson Ltd, 181A High Holborn,
London WC1V 7QX

First published in the United States of America
in 2020 by Thames & Hudson Inc., 500 Fifth Avenue,
New York, New York 10110

Wild Kitchen: Nature-Loving Chefs at Home © 2020
Thames & Hudson Ltd, London
Text © 2020 Claire Bingham
For the recipe credits, please see page 221.
For the picture credits, please see page 221.

British Library Cataloguing-in-Publication Data
A catalogue record for this book is available
from the British Library

Library of Congress Control Number 2020932678

ISBN 978-0-500-02301-3

Printed and bound in China by 1010 Printing International Ltd

Be the first to know about our new releases,
exclusive content and author events by visiting
thamesandhudson.com
thamesandhudsonusa.com
thamesandhudson.com.au